ALTERNATIVE FUTURES FOR WORSHIP
General Introduction

ALTERNATIVE FUTURES FOR WORSHIP

Volume 1
General Introduction

Volume Editor

REGIS A. DUFFY, O.F.M.

Authors

MICHAEL A. COWAN
PAUL J. PHILIBERT, O.P.
EDWARD J. KILMARTIN, S.J.

THE LITURGICAL PRESS
Collegeville, Minnesota 56321

Cover design by Mary Jo Pauly

Manufactured in the United States of America.

ISBN 0-8146-1493-0

	2	3	4	5	6	7	8

Library of Congress Cataloging-in-Publication Data

Alternative futures for worship.

Includes bibliographies.
Contents: v. 1. General Introduction / volume editor, Regis A. Duffy ; authors, Michael A. Cowan, Paul J. Philibert, Edward J. Kilmartin — v. 2. Baptism and confirmation / edited by Mark Searle ; by Andrew D. Thompson . . . [et al.] — v. 3. The eucharist / edited by Bernard J. Lee ; by Thomas Richstatter . . . [et al.] — [etc.]
1. Sacraments (Liturgy) 2. Catholic Church—Liturgy. I. Lee, Bernard J., 1932–
BX2200.A49   1987   265   86-27300
ISBN 0-8146-1491-4 (set)

CONTENTS

THE CONTRIBUTORS

BERNARD J. LEE, S.M., a member of the department of graduate theology at St. Mary's University (San Antonio), has published *The Becoming of the Church, Religious Experience and Process Theology* (with Harry Cargas) and *Dangerous Memories: House Churches and Our American Story* (with Michael A. Cowan).

REGIS A. DUFFY, O.F.M., is professor of theology, The Washington Theological Union, Silver Spring, Maryland.

MICHAEL A. COWAN is adjunct professor of pastoral theology in the school of theology of St. John's University in Collegeville and in the school of divinity of The College of St. Thomas in St. Paul. He is co-author (with Bernard J. Lee) of *Dangerous Memories: House Churches and Our American Story.*

PAUL J. PHILIBERT, O.P., is president of the Dominican School of Philosophy and Theology in the Graduate Theology Union at Berkeley, California.

EDWARD J. KILMARTIN, S.J., is professor of theology, The Pontifical Oriental Institute, Rome, and a member of the Oriental-Roman Catholic Dialogue.

INTRODUCTION TO THE SERIES

Bernard J. Lee, S.M.

A Dream

This book and the series which it introduces began with a dream. That is probably the place to start.

Some years ago, in what seems like another age, I was a doctoral student at Graduate Theological Union in Berkeley. This was during the sixties and early seventies. Those were tense, painful, and glorious years when passions ran high and dreams were the order of the day. One Saturday evening a group of students and friends gathered together for a eucharist in one of our residences that was followed by a potluck supper and conversation late into the evening. Someone proposed a fantasy: there is a ten million dollar fund which will be awarded to the finest dream about how to enable a religion to make a difference in how the world goes; what is your plan? We broke into small groups for a while, then came back together to vote on the winning dream. The group I was in dreamed the winning dream. It was to find a place in the world where thirty-nine people could live for an indefinite period of time and have an environment that would be conducive to the assigned task. Let me indicate the personnel required and their job description:

two Scripture scholars
two liturgists
two sacramental theologians
two historians
two anthropologists

two sociologists
two psychologists
two classical composers
two popular folk composers
two singers
two novelists
two poets
two dramatists
two circus clowns
two artists
two architects
two pray-ers, one a mystic
two devils (because the real world should be significantly
represented)
three saints (three, because they should have a slight edge
over the devils).

The job description was to be: "Live together in community. Work, pray, play, fight, sing, dance, eat, and drink together. You are to explore with your lived experiences and combined intuitions how contemporary people can worship in the deep midst of perhaps the most complex and challenging of historical eras ever. Their worship must help transform their world. You may not leave until the job is completed."

Some of us in the small discussion group who were interested in process theology had become familiar as students with the philosophy of Alfred North Whitehead. We had read and believed his remarks that

> The power of God is the worship He inspires. That religion is strong which in its ritual and its modes of thought evokes an apprehension of the commanding vision. The worship of God is not a rule of safety—it is an adventure of the spirit, a flight after the unattainable. The death of religion comes with the repression of the high hope of adventure.[1]

Others of us had read and believed the work of cultural anthropologist, Clifford Geertz. We were convinced by him of the deep, symbiotic relationship between faith and culture and the power of religion to give meaning to all proximate acts:

> It is [the] placing of proximate acts in ultimate contexts that makes religion, frequently at least, socially so powerful.[2]

If God is up to something in history, then religion should make an appreciable difference to the face history wears. Worship cannot be indifferent to that transformative power which comes from God and goes into all the nooks and crannies of our personal and corporate histories.

That real dream which won the unreal ten million dollars got tucked away like most dreams.

Several years later, as I was crossing the campus at St. John's University in Collegeville, Minnesota, one morning, I met Fr. Daniel Durken, O.S.B., who had just been named director of The Liturgical Press. As we chatted, Daniel spoke of his interest in new authors, new materials, and new projects for The Press. Several days later I phoned him for a lunch date, and there over the noon table I hauled out the dream. It was tempered by a little economic realism: ten million dollars was not our starting point!

In the intervening years since the original fantasy, the dream has been validated for me as a right kind of dream. I still believe that the personnel named in our dream are vital to the enhancement of worship as God's power in the world. But if the whole dream cannot be done at once, then it should still be done piece by piece. A strong liaison between liturgy, theology, and the human sciences is a powerful "piece" of the dream with which to begin.

Daniel expressed an interest in this project as a possibility for The Press. I formulated an initial proposal. Daniel, the late John Dwyer, business manager for The Press (1952–1986), and I sat together a number of times, critiquing the proposal as it went through several drafts. We decided to seek a broader perspective, so I began to contact liturgists and sacramental theologians in this country for critical interaction. The support was strong, animated, and immediate.

I invited a number of men and women who are prominent in sacramental and liturgical theology to become members of the editorial board. I was saddened that the women who were invited when the board was formed were already in such demand that their commitments did not permit them to be members at that time. They were and have been helpful numerous times with suggestions and encouragement. The original board members were: Bernard Cooke (College of the Holy Cross), Regis Duffy (Washington Theological Union), Peter Fink (Weston School of Theology), and Mark Searle (University of Notre Dame). We met for a long weekend in the Chicago area. The meeting (rare for a meeting!) was sheer delight. Gradually we forged a working description for the project. "Forged" is an accurate image because it was hard, hard work. There were so many fascinating visions, so many ways we might go. A proposal emerged out of our energetic discussions which we continued to critique and improve by correspondence. Several months later we met again in Chicago to agree on how we would proceed.

It soon became apparent to me that the project we were undertaking meant that the editorial board should also have membership from the human sciences. Consequently Michael Cowan (St. John's University) became an active member of the board. Since then Jennifer Glen and Irene Nowell have become members of the editorial board, with the particular task of editing all of the alternative rituals that appear in the series.

No matter how well a project is described ahead of time, it is not possible to foresee and cover every issue that will arise. I cannot express enough my gratitude to the board members for continuing critical interaction, sometimes quite animated, as the project evolved.

So that is how the dream got going. Each volume in the series is edited by a member of the editorial board. Each of those editors had the responsibility of forming a team of authors for each volume. Some thirty women and men authors have contributed their expertise, inventiveness, and collaborative energies to the project, *Alternative Futures for Worship*. It has not been an easy task at all. We have looked for team members who are recognized in their disciplines and able to collaborate on interdisciplinary work. Now anyone who has seriously attempted sustained interdisciplinary research and writing knows how incredibly difficult and meticulous this work is, not to say painful at times as well. Careful listening is difficult enough within the confines of one's own discipline, but when we cross disciplines and try to hear one another *on each other's own grounds*, the complexity and challenge increase geometrically. However, the cumulative richness of shared intuition and mutually informed instinct makes the pain and panic a small price to pay!

Each team of authors for each volume met together near the beginning of the work, usually after preliminary exchanges and drafts. The faith of The Liturgical Press in the project is incredibly tangible in the financial support for team meetings, two meetings for the editorial board, and seven other meetings for the team of authors for each volume. That has meant hotel arrangements, meals, and travel from all over the country. Critical interaction during the writing was continuous; so was the struggle, and ultimately the satisfaction. Each team of authors was facilitated by a member of the editorial board, and each volume has had the ongoing critical interaction from a second reader who was also a member of the editorial board. We know that what we are doing is the right thing to be doing. We are also deeply aware that it is but a beginning.

There are at least four sound reasons for attempting a project like *Alternative Futures for Worship* that are future-oriented reasons. They are reasons that have to do with religion in the making. There is still another future-oriented reason that is a particularly difficult and risky one. This fifth reason is somewhat different from the first four.

The sixth reason is a present-oriented reason, but intimately related to the other five. What possible difference does a *possible future moment* make for a *pressing present moment?* Why should anyone in the white heat of daily pastoral exigencies sit down in the quiet cool of evening to read and think about *Alternative Futures for Worship?* How do future and present come together in the life of a pastoral minister?

Christian faith is deeply eschatological: it always faces a future and a kingdom to come. However, Christian thinkers point out that eschaton does not mean, as we once understood, "the four last things," all of which are later than the now in which we live each day. What is coming already makes a claim upon the present. In fact the future is given a present "presence" when it is allowed to shape people's lived experience. Therefore, *Alternative Futures for Worship* is not just about what might happen someday; it is about future scenarios that impinge upon today.

Frankly, such talk about the *eschaton* is but a convoluted and metaphorical way of saying that this project has immense pastoral implications. The implications are *not* the alternative rituals that are being wondered into existence. The implications are the transformations that can happen within the heart and mind of any pastoral minister, the deeper understandings of the human situation towards which the redemptive love of God is directed in all the sacramental life of the Church. In short, the way is open now for the deeper humanization of our life of worship. Each volume in this series in its own way proposes that deeper humanization, and for that, no one need wait for tomorrow.

The Four Future-Oriented Reasons

Liturgical Reform as Continuous Event

Our project is not merely a response to the needs of a particular historical moment. *Alternative Futures for Worship* addresses a perennial situation. During most of the Church's history, liturgical reform has been characterized by fevered sprints after long periods of inactivity. That is as unhealthy for a social body as for an individual human body.

It is not as though our life of worship has been fully and adequately updated, and now we are enjoying it. The liturgical reform following the Second Vatican Council has been an immense gift to Christian communities in both form and vision (such as the Rite of Christian Initiation for Adults). But there is no reason for complacency. It is clear, for example, that the revised sacrament of reconciliation has not succeeded in any significant way in calling Christians into its experience. It is too facile to say, "people have lost their sense of sin." Our age is often deeply anguished, and the world is not riding upon a crest of optimism. The rite does not seem to have been able to locate the cry of our age clearly and tangibly upon the horizon of ultimacy. Or to take another example, the rite of Christian marriage is far from having reckoned with the feminist critique. There is much work to do in the present, as well as mustering active imagination for the future of Christian worship, which is the orientation of this project.

The Church has long understood itself to be *semper reformanda*, in need of continual transformation. But it has not yet structured itself to provide for the future of worship through sustained and continuous research and committed, relentless experiment. This project intends to be a "for instance" of what continuous and sustained exploration might look like. It is indeed an unofficial "for instance." None of the alternatives we "wonder" into existence is intended for actual use. We simply hope that what we offer will stimulate interest in and commitment to responsible and imaginative exploration.

The functions of pure and applied research are taken for granted in our contemporary society. Pure research attempts to formulate the best in theoretical understandings. It knows that its proposals are always subject to adjustment, elaboration, refinement, and sometimes revision. We value "think tanks."

Applied research stems from a passionate commitment to explore what actual differences those theoretical understandings might make for our lived experience. This is the area of technological research. It has an almost profligate character. Its storehouse of alternatives is overstocked with more possibilities than can ever be used.

Such superabundance is vital to the creative transformation of human life. There should be a lavishness about the resources and options available ahead of time. It is an expression of hope for the future. *Alternative Futures for Worship* is an expression of such hope for the future. It is our version of both pure and applied research: forging the best theoretical understandings we can and imaginatively exploring their consequences for the public prayer life of the Church.

We who are involved in this project feel that by actively maintaining a storehouse of ritual alternatives, there is a better chance of keeping worship forms and life forms mutually engaged.

The first good reason for this project, then, is our conviction that worship is important enough to the life of the world that the search for its best comprehension and best expressions must be continual.

EMPIRICALLY COMMITTED THEOLOGY

Good theology has always been a faithful reflection of faith experience. Fidelity to experience is a touchstone of valid theological reflection. It is commonplace today to recognize that the human sciences are a report upon experience and that theology must take serious cognizance of that report.

Each of the sacraments deals with some particular "slice of life." Some "piece of ordinary human experience" is pried open through ritual so that its potential to mediate religious experience is exploited: food, eating, and table fellowship; water, cleansing, birth, initiation, and socialization processes; marriage and family; alienation and reconciliation, and so forth. All of those human experiences that are foundational to the Church's sacramental system have been observed, reported upon, generalized, interpreted. In a word we have become more deliberately empirical. One of the marks of our age in Western culture, especially this century, is the systematic way in which we attempt to describe and interpret human experience.

The *Alternative Futures for Worship* project arises out of a strong commitment to listen seriously and critically to the various reports of the human sciences and then open sacramental theology to a profound internal relationship with the human sciences.

There is no single, univocal report from the human sciences on any area of human life. This must be kept in mind. For example, one cannot simply speak of the stages of development in a person's life; one must speak of that development as formulated by Piaget,

or Kohlberg, or Erikson, or Gilligan. They may not be contradic-
tory, but they never say exactly the same thing. Therefore, in each
volume we attempt to name clearly the particular voices from the
human sciences to which we are attending. That is, of course, a
limitation. However, we try to dialogue with mainstream figures
whose positions have a reasonably broad acceptance. Since it is not
possible to dialogue with all the voices, the only options to being
selective are to ignore those voices altogether or to be fearsomely
eclectic. Theological dialogue with the human sciences is too critical to ignore. Therefore, in all the volumes of this series, we try
to be clear about our selection of resources, even as we know that
there are other legitimate and helpful resources to be explored. In
none of the volumes are we saying that our proposals are proffered
as normative recommendations for *what* sacramental theology
should hold. We hope in each case, however, to be a good instance
of *how* that and other dialogues might fruitfully occur. It is a modest
proposal.

The second good reason, then, for this project is that an active
relation between theology and the human sciences helps faith reflection keep firmly tied to experiential bases.

UNDERSTANDING AS "CONSTRUCTION"

There is still a larger and perhaps more urgent consideration
that compels theology to attend to the human sciences. The human
sciences do not merely report upon experience but they participate
in the creation of the experience upon which they report. It is not
that there is a kind of "objective" human nature upon which all
the human sciences offer their varied perspectives and against which
they can be adjudicated for accuracy. Accurate knowledge is not
a mirror of objective fact. Out of an interaction between someone
who knows and something that is known, knowledge is concretely
constructed. What is constructed is not merely a formal resemblance
between knower and known. The knowledge is a new "fact," getting some of its character from the subjectivity of the subject and
some from the objectivity of the object. That "fact" is clothed with
feeling, weighted with value, and replete with meaning. Human
knowing does not find meaning readymade. Our quest for
knowledge and meaning is always an active engagement in the social construction of reality.

Women and men who have entered seriously into the feminist
movement, for example, have not merely understood themselves

differently. Their selves are made into different selves by a change
in the meaning structures to which they give power. How such
people go about being human changes significantly. Families that
enter into therapy in a family systems context do not merely reunder-
stand the "already" of their lives; together they co-create a new
mode of family existence.

It is not only the professionals in the human sciences for whom
this is true. In our culture there is a broad exposure to systems that
come out of the human sciences. One can get it in *Psychology Today*
and meet it almost weekly in *Time* and *Newsweek*. Young people
get it from their teachers in classrooms. Many people hear it from
the pulpit, even if not in terms of technical categories. You can even
get a burgeoning sense of systems theory in "Cathy," "Sally Forth,"
and "Momma" in the daily comics.

We are not accustomed to thinking of our systems of thought
as creators of the worlds we inhabit. We have traditionally thought
of our systems as reflecting them, but not making them. Because
this is such a crucial matter, I want to restate it from the perspectives of sociology and hermeneutics.

Peter Berger speaks about the unfinished character of the human organism. Nonhuman animals are born with a specialized instinctual structure that relates them to their world. But that is not
true for human animals for whom culture and not genes helps them
build the human worlds of meaning that they will inhabit. Culture
is both the name of the world we build and of the ongoing process
of building it. All our studies and disciplines are part of the cultural work by which we produce a world and "finish" our own human being. Thus Berger refrains from positing a content to human
nature, except to say that it is human nature to produce the worlds
we inhabit. "What appears at any particular moment as 'human
nature' is itself a product of man's world-building activity."[3]

The human sciences and theology are both cultural phenomena
which participate in the business of world construction. Because
of Christian faith's commitments to the creative transformation of
human life—which is an act of world construction—its partnership
with the human sciences is a "holy alliance" (or should be!).

Hermeneutical theory has stressed a similar point. We never
come neutral and naked into a new experience. Every experience
is already and immediately clothed with perspective and interpretation that reflect the past history we carry with us. We always have
preunderstandings that condition each new perception, each new

act of interpreting experience. David Tracy writes that "every interpreter enters into the act of interpretation bearing the history of the effects, conscious and unconscious, of the traditions to which we all ineluctably belong."[4] The theologian who reflects systematically upon faith experience is influenced not only by the long tradition of faith in his or her bones but by the presuppositions about human reality that belong to her or his contemporary frames of reference. Those presuppositions enter participatively into the interpreted experience. There is no uninterpreted "fact"; the interpreter always impinges upon the interpreted. In a word something in us contributes to the construction of fact.

Whether we are largely conscious of it or not, the human sciences in either their technical states or their popularized versions condition greatly our sense of what it means to be a human person. They do not just condition but concretely help build what it means to be human. Thus when we say that the sacraments all deal with slices of human life, we must acknowledge that those slices are partly constructed in meaning by the human sciences of our age. When theology keeps in close dialogue with the human sciences, there is a better chance of becoming aware of the forces in the world which are helping create human meaning. Though we can never raise all our presuppositions to clear consciousness.

Like the human sciences theology itself is one of the constructing agents in the world. Sometimes it assumes a countercultural role when it places certain meanings of human life under suspicion. Faith has its own deep convictions about human values and seeks natural liaisons with the human sciences that help it in its construction work. Sometimes, however, it is the human sciences which rightly place theological interpretations under suspicion and send theology back to the drawing boards. What goes on between theology and social sciences has the nature of mutual conversation. "Conversion" is Hans-Georg Gadamer's image for the continuing acts of interpretation through which we construct our meaning worlds.[5] Sometimes the conversation is friendly and affirming; sometimes it has a sharp edge and involves risk.

The third good reason then for this project is the importance of conversation between theology and the social sciences because of the role each plays in constructing the worlds we inhabit. The conversation is too important to be left to happenstance.

Playing with Possibility as an Act of Care

The first good reason for this project which I named was that the reform of liturgy should be a continuous concern. I named the importance for the vitality of any organization of having a whole warehouse profligately stocked with fascinating possibilities. At one level, of course, this is a matter of survival. Organizations that plan well live both longer and more interestingly. At another level disciplined imagination is an act of care. As best as we can, we do not leave to random evolution the events that matter deeply to us. We think of all the interesting and powerful ways that a tale might be told. We do that precisely because we care very much. This project is an expression of care about the many tales that might be told.

The name of this project is *Alternative Futures for Worship*. The alternative futures are rituals that we are wondering into existence to exemplify the consequences of positions taken when theology and the human sciences converse seriously. Why not just offer theological reflection? Why wonder rituals into existence? The answer to those questions reflects the fourth good reason for this project.

Only a small percentage of Catholics has studied the history or theologies of the Second Vatican Council. Yet the configuration of the Church is very different today because of that council. The differences are not just cosmetic. Even though most people have not systematically studied that council's presuppositions about Church and about human history, its perceptions have gradually seeped into our spiritual centers. How? While there are multiple answers to the "how," certainly one of the most crucial is the liturgy of the Church. Even though general absolution is not widespread, its possibility and occasional usage tell a new story about the communal character of sin and grace. The transposition of the confession of sins from an anonymously dark little room to face-to-face interaction bespeaks a different sense of both community leadership (priest) and community membership (penitent). Removing the altar from the back wall so that it begins to look like a table in the midst of a community brings the notion of eucharistic meal to the forefront. Before long people wanted bread to look like bread again, and the sacred vessels to look like a plate and a cup. The use of the words chalice and paten recedes. Once the language of worship becomes the vernacular and people sing and pray more interactively, the language about the priest saying Mass begins to disappear. People and priest together celebrate the Eucharist; the priest does not "say Mass" alone. The point is that liturgy is one of the crucial places where the Church's self-understanding expresses itself and seeps into Christian consciousness. Worship is where new understandings make a formidable appearance. Liturgy is where the consequences of the Second Vatican Council have been singularly telling.

In the early part of this century, William James suggested the importance of knowing what consequences something has in order to know what it means. "All realities influence our practice, and that influence is their meaning for us."[6] If in their dialogue sacramental theology and the human sciences arrive at some positions, those positions have consequences. If those positions garner assent from both the heart and head of Christian believers, they will have consequences in our lives of prayer and worship. When we wonder alternative rituals into existence, therefore, we are doing so to help understand more fully the meaning of the dialogue between human sciences and theology. As James says, if you really want to know the "cash value" of any idea, "set it at work within the stream of your experience."[7] One of the best ways to know the "cash value" of any sacramental theology is to put that theology to work in the stream of liturgical experience.

All of the alternative rituals proposed in this series are means of exploring the meaning of the dialogue we have undertaken. They are all unfinished, tentative, speculative essays upon meaning. None of them is suggested for actual use anywhere. This is not "an underground mass book." We cannot insist strongly enough upon that point. The rites proffered in these volumes are nothing more and nothing less than attempts on the part of people who care to use disciplined imagination to explore Christian meanings.

In our daily lives we try to take the resources of the present moment and make the best decisions we can that do honor to both our remembered past and our anticipated future. There is never just a past; it is always a remembered past in which memory concretely shapes what we are calling the past. There is never just a future; it is always an anticipated future in which anticipation concretely shapes what we are calling the future. Anticipation is a way in which our understanding spreads our very lives out before us to build our tomorrows, our next years, and perhaps even the kingdom of God. The anticipatory spreading out of our lives is an intrinsic part of how we understand anything and everything. Anticipation is not a mere exercise in fantasy, it is an essential piece of how we understand. Martin Heidegger, the German philosopher whose work has given contemporary work in hermeneutics much of its inspiration, has suggested the term "projection" in his discussion of interpretation. We do not simply understand something *first* and only *then* project possibilities. Understanding itself projects.

Most of us who read and explore the fascicles of the *Alternative Futures for Worship* series are Christians for whom worship is an essential activity about which we care deeply. If worship is a constitutive expression of our faith, then our understandings of God, our world, and ourselves must often involve worship projections. Only people who do not care would refrain from tenderness toward their own future. Thus, what we are attempting to do at a more conscious level in this series is project Christian life liturgically on the basis of understandings that are being built out of the conversation between theology and the human sciences, and we are doing it because *it matters.* This may be a labored way of making a simple point, but the issue is clear, I hope. We are not offering alternative rituals for anyone's liturgical use in today's Church. We are engaging in the act of understanding our sacramental life with care. The projection that is intrinsic to the act of understanding is what we are trying to embody in the alternative rituals that we wonder into existence.

The fourth good reason for this project, then, has to do with the proffering of alternative ritual forms. We have chosen to do this because it is a vivid way of "seeing" what kind of world the dialogue between the human sciences and sacramental and liturgical theology constructs. These alternatives help us feel what difference it all makes. The projection of possible scenarios is itself an act of hope. It is a way of taking care of a precious possession.

One Future-Oriented Risky Reason

PLAYING WITH POSSIBILITY AS AN ACT OF FAITH

I have named four reasons that we who are working on this series feel are good solid reasons for *Alternative Futures for Worship.* Yet we acknowledge that it is in someways foolhardy and risky and presumptuous to sit down at a table and write rituals. The symbolic world of the religious psyche is not under rational, propositional control. Our symbols know more about us than we know about them. Rituals well up out of the depths of experience; they cannot be conjured up on the spot. Only those rituals have power which resonate profoundly with the symbolic structure of the spiritual life. Rituals only "work" if they have symbiotic connectedness with a people's deep story. Rituals are incubated in the womb of our deeper experiences, and here we surely include the unconscious and the incredible ways in which it knows us, knows God, and knows the world.

This, then, is still another reason why it is clear to us that we are not proposing rituals for experimental use anyplace. We are *probing* ritual life, not *proposing* ritual life for anybody's use. We are saying that "if such and such a position emerging from the human sciences/theology dialogue looks promising, let us be as concrete as we can get and imagine aspects of its ritual expression." Often our point is not whether a finished new alternative ritual is a polished response to insights into human experience from the human sciences but whether we have made helpful initial suggestions about viable directions for continuing exploration.

If it is risky to play with the sacred forms of public worship, it is probably riskier in the long run not to play with them. Liturgy has to do with life. Erik Erikson has demonstrated effectively that play is an essential developmental dynamic in which a child tries out the roles it will one day have to fulfill. Playfulness invokes qualities of imagination without which life and love die of heaviness. It is no mere play on words to say that wondering future alternatives into existence is an intrinsic act of wonderment. Wonderment is a response to wonderful things. If liturgy is not a wonderful event that evokes wonderment in our beholding, it is hardly an act of faith. As Abraham Heschel has said, faith emerges precisely when we begin to ponder who and what lit the wonder of our eyes. Because liturgical life is a growing, living thing, playing with possible futures is not simply wonderment about faith, it is an act of faith.

The Immediacy of Present-Oriented Reasons

What Now?—Pastoral Implications

So far the reasons given for this project have been mostly future-oriented reasons. That is, after all, the project's thrust. But it has been an education for me in the present. And that is a story I have heard over and over from those who have been cooperating to make the project become a reality. For all of us, it has been a shared experience in teaching and learning in the present time as our disparate disciplines have rubbed off on each other.

I have been deeply involved in this project for over five years. During this time I have also been teaching men and women preparing for both nonordained and ordained ministries. I have as well often been a sacramental minister myself. As general editor for the series, I have read and interacted with all the manuscripts as they came in, in first drafts and in multiple revisions. As a result of the "education" I received from this, I have revised in major ways the courses I offer in sacramental theology. But I have also revised in significant ways the self of the sacramental minister which I sometimes am. In short, I believe that the rewards of "plowing through" this series are considerable for the present life of the Church.

The Humanization of Liturgy

I deliberately speak of "plowing through" and not just "reading through" the volumes of this series, because the project often means turning over the earth upon which we trod and out of which we are made. The Latin word for earth is *humus*. The Latin word for the human person is a derivative of that; so also is the Latin adjective that refers to that earthbound being, *humanus*. All the human sciences are, each in its own way, a plowing of the earth of humanity. A lot of humanity is plowed in the seven volumes of this series. A considerable education awaits anyone who carefully encounters the whole of the series. Much of the best in contemporary understandings of the meaning and nature of human experience is to be found herein. The bibliographies give more than ample help to anyone who wishes to continue the exploration and the education.

The faith of the Judaeo-Christian tradition affirms that all the world reflects God, and in particular the human being is made in the image of divine being. To know more about the human person whose existence is exposed to the transformative power of God in all sacraments is also to know more about the transformative ways of God's redemptive love.

Many times now as a Christian minister I have been with people with serious illness (not necessarily terminal illness). Not only people with weak faith but those with great faith find the meanings out of which they have lived successfully for many years breaking down when brought face to face with their finitude. Sometime ago I encountered Ernest Becker's *The Birth and Death of Meaning*, and *The Denial of Death*. However, in Jennifer Glen's contribution to the volume on the anointing of the sick, I saw this sacrament located within the context of "deconstructed" and reconstructed meaning, and I saw reconstructed meaning presented under the rubric of redeemed experience, precisely as the efficacy of the sacrament of anointing. That may not be the total explanation of the sacrament, of course, but it is a true one. The sacrament of anointing can easily be an accomplice in the denial of death, rather than a facilitator of the reconstruction of the meaning of being God's creature, that is, of being finite. To be a creature is to be a finite, limited being, and our finitude must be embraced and redeemed, not escaped.

My intention is not to summarize that volume before anyone reads it. I want to say that in my work as general editor, I have often found not just a new theological synthesis, but sometimes a new pastoral soul. I do not promise, however, instant transformation into "formidable pastor" for anyone! I am just noting my experience and my conviction that the dialogue with the human sciences is pastorally fertile. Since grappling with some of the materials in the anointing volume, for example, I have ministered to finitude, within myself and within others whose world of meaning has been violated (whether by illness or for other reasons). I recognize personally that the shape of my ministry and my ministering self has undergone significant shifts because of having been humanized by the dialogue between theology and the human sciences. When I wonder existentially about the tale *to be told* (the alternative futures), invariably the *tale being told* becomes new. Even if the words of the sacrament of anointing remain the same, the experience of the sacrament has many faces, depending upon what manner of humanization is the stage upon which the sacramental drama is set. I gave but one example from my personal experience. They could be multiplied.

The Presence of the Future

In his published sermon on "Waiting," Paul Tillich stressed that whenever we wait earnestly for someone or something, it already has power over us while we wait.[8] The present moment of waiting gets some of its configuration from the shape of that for which we wait. If I am waiting for someone, my mood while I am waiting is shaped by the relationship I have with the person for whom I wait and by what I surmise our encounter will feel like when we meet. The one for whom I wait is already making a difference in my life as I wait and because I wait.

If this is true, then the future is important to immediate experience. All those possibles which I entertain with enthusiasm shape how I perceive the present and what I do in the present—at least there is that strong possibility. The contrast between what is and what might be energizes the present. There is always the danger, of course, of forsaking the present for the not yet. And that is surely not what I am suggesting as a benefit of the sacramental future. I am thinking rather of how possibilities that hold out promise bend back upon the present and pave the highways into the future starting from now.

For example, the fascicle on initiation begins with a remarkable report from the human sciences upon the primordial role of immediate family in the identity formation of a child, and that includes of course the child's religious identity. Yet the role of family is barely ritualized in the rites of initiation. However, a community that understands the centrality of the family will have a different sense of what is happening when it initiates its children and when it symbolizes its processes of initiation in the rites of initiation.

In a chapter in the introductory volume, Michael Cowan cites some of the work of Clifford Geertz on rituals as "models of" and "models for" life. An effective ritual connects us into the story that is being lived (model "of"), but also provides a sort of template for how we shall live (model "for"). The current rite of initiation that is used for infant baptism is neither a model of or a model for the behavior of parents as the fundamental matrix for their child's socialization into Christian identity. Even short of having ritual forms that are a more faithful response to how religious identity is usually formed, the community that knows the centrality of family along with a minister who also knows have leeway to give some shape to the celebration. That is even truer in the ritual for adults in which the rubrics often indicate that the minister says "these or similar words." There is much to be done now that better information about the human condition can be combined with liturgical sensitivity.

My Story Is Being Heard!

Too often theological concerns and pastoral issues seem worlds apart. It is a sad history that has allowed a lot of theology to become so disengaged from the human story that people exposed to theology do not hear their own stories told. Theology's concern may be the experience of God, but its always the human experience of God.

In *A Rumor of Angels* religious sociologist Peter Berger says that our starting point is always daily experience. Only when we find in our ordinary experience "signals of transcendence," may we proceed to religious affirmations.[9] God is found in our world or nowhere for us. The data of theological reflection are the appearances of God in the world. The religious discourse of theology that maintains its experiential moorings is redolent of the human experiences which mediate God's worldly appearances. This is especially true of sacramental theology. Ordinary events, daily experience, the heights and depths of the human condition: these are the bearer's of God's presence.

I want to suggest, therefore, the advantages of sacramental theology, which pays serious attention to the report upon human experience that comes from the empirical social sciences. First, if the world that harbors the appearances of God makes a direct appearance in our theological language, there is more possibility of some immediacy of assent. People can more easily say: I recognize that story as mine, and the signals of transcendence as plausible. Second, if the theology of sacrament or liturgy is not only an accurate report upon our experience of God, but upon the kind of human experience that is sacramental of God, that theology gives clues about how to live religiously and humanly. The theological and pastoral are not two different worlds.

For example, in the fascicle on ministries, there is a sustained discussion of the nature of leadership and the exercise of power. Of the many possible ways in which power can be exercised, some specific choices are made by the New Testament. And only to the extent that the presbyterate functions according to the relational model of power is it truly a living sacrament of the kingdom. The use of sociological categories by James and Evelyn Whitehead evokes experiences of community that many of us recognize. Those categories are integrated into the theology of Christian leadership, so that the theology itself is pastoral through and through: it attends carefully to the human condition of God's redemptive presence.

In a word, one of the pastoral benefits of work like this is catechetical in character. It becomes easier to tell the story of a sacrament so that people stand a better chance of seeing their own stories unfurl. For people who live incarnational theology, the stories of deity and humanity are not identical, but neither are they disparate, for "in the world" is where God is for us.

The Structure of ALTERNATIVE FUTURES FOR WORSHIP

There are seven volumes in the *Alternative Futures for Worship* series. The first volume addresses general areas of sacramental life, especially symbolic and ritual action. Baptism and

Confirmation are dealt with together in a single volume. There is a separate fascicle for each of the remaining sacraments.

There is a similar structure to each of the fascicles. However, the exact format for each presentation varies from volume to volume. The differences reflect the particular ways in which each team in its considerable dialogue fashioned its work. Those differences are a richness. If format differs from volume to volume, there is clearly a common commitment throughout, and these are its elements:

1. Let us listen to some of the reporting from the human sciences upon the principal life experiences to which a particular sacrament attends.

2. Let us take serious theological account of that report.

3. In the light of that report and our theological response, let us reflect upon historical aspects of each sacrament's heritage in Christian practice.

4. Let us have the audacity to wonder about ritual reflections of a sacramental life construed as we have done in our dialogue between the human sciences and sacramental theology.

Our goal is not to produce a new sacramental theology and a new sacramentary. We do hope to think theologically about sacrament and liturgy and about the pastoral needs of today's and tomorrow's Church. We desire to recognize the kind of conversation needed to enhance our ritual life and to "for instance" it. We believe that Christian experience addresses history head on, that it offers the world redeemed experience. We believe that this is so important that we have assembled multiple teams of some of this nation's best talent and asked them to care together and out loud.

We make only modest claims about our achievement. There are no feelings of finality about any position proposed. We are sometimes struggling out loud in print, not for the ideal formulation, but for fruitful ways to "do theology" and to live a life of worship that makes the world a better sacrament of the marvels of God's love.

Footnotes

1. Alfred North Whitehead, *Science and the Modern World* (New York: Macmillan, 1925) 268–269.

2. Clifford Geertz, *The Interpretation of Culture* (New York: Basic Books, 1973) 122. This chapter first appeared in 1966 in another publication.

3. Peter Berger, *The Sacred Canopy*, (Garden City, N.Y.: Doubleday, 1969) 7. See the entire first chapter on "Religion and World Construction."

4. David Tracy and Robert Grant, *A Short History of the Interpretation of the Bible* (Philadelphia: Fortress, 1984) 156.

5. Hans-Georg Gadamer, *Truth and Method* (New York: Crossroads, 1965) 330ff.

6. William James, *Pragmatism* (New York: Meridian, 1955) 44.

7. *Ibid.* 46.

8. Paul Tillich, *Shaking of the Foundations* (London: Penguin, 1962) 153.

9. Peter Berger, *A Rumor of Angels* (Garden City, N.Y.: Doubleday 1970) chapter 2, passim.

INTRODUCTION

Regis A. Duffy, O.F.M.

"Sacraments in general" is a familiar title to anyone who studied theology before the Second Vatican Council. Such a course presents a systematic reflection on the rich sacramental heritage of the Church. Although only individual sacraments actually exist, "sacraments in general" remains an attempt to abstract and to delineate the communality that all sacraments share. The danger of such an abstraction is, however, that we can forget that sacraments are not about theory but about a Spirit-empowered experience of Christ within his community, the Church. Also, sacraments cannot be discussed apart from the present mission of the Church and its ultimate goal, the Kingdom of God.

The student of the history of "sacraments in general" will be surprised by the diversity and complexity of theological theories about sacrament over the centuries.[1] But the largely unexplored complementary area of sacramental *praxis* during these centuries sometimes seems to be alienated from sacramental theory of the same period. When the brilliant sacramental systems of St. Thomas Aquinas in the thirteenth century or of Duns Scotus in the fourteenth century, for example, are compared with the pastoral *praxis* of sacraments in these same periods, this separation between theory and *praxis* can be seen in startling relief. The wide disparity between the dogmatic discussions on sacraments and the pastoral sessions on the use and abuse of sacraments at the Council of Trent in the sixteenth century is another example of the split between theory and *praxis*.

Such a split is more than a recognition that the real and the ideal can be quite different in a pastoral situation. It may, in fact, indicate a lack of ministerial awareness in the actual operational definitions of sacraments in a parish in contrast to the theory that is heard in homilies and religious education courses in that same community.

These remarks preface an important reminder to the reader of this book: insightful sacramental theory, whether interdisciplinary or not, does not necessarily beget a renewed sacramental *praxis*. Readers must be active participants, if the discussions in this book are to be helpful in renewing the sacramental ministries of their churches. This participation entails a sharpened awareness of the current sacramental *praxis* in the reader's ministerial situation. The contributors in this book did not set out to write solutions for sacramental situations of our time. Rather, they provide a better vantage point from which readers can perceive how sacramental theory and *praxis* merge or clash in their own pastoral situations.

The three chapters in this book might be compared to a classical symphony with three movements. Each movement often is structured in a different form but there is an overarching unity to the symphony. The very differences in content and form of each movement ultimately contribute to this sense of musical cohesion. In similar fashion the unity of sacramental concerns in this book has been achieved by the writers' different perspectives, which are a result of their respective academic disciplines. The careful reader will note, however, that there is a unifying motif throughout these three chapters, that of *communication*.

This is not surprising when we remember that God's communication and our response are at the core of the sacramental event. Communication implies a sharing of *meaning*. God's welcomed meaning as actualized in Christ and continually made present by the action of the Spirit shapes the values and priorities of our current lives in view of God's future reign. Christian meaning has never ceased to be formed and reformed by God's complementary Word and sacrament.

This fact suggests additional questions to the reader of these chapters: in what ways does Christian meaning as communicated through sacramental word and action challenge both the community and the individual to appropriate more fully the "good news" of Christ? How do our socioeconomic and cultural contexts color sacramental meaning and communication? How capable of participation in symbol must a Christian be if the meanings of sacrament are not to be distorted? Is our local Church giving sacraments or is it sacrament?

With these questions in mind, the reader may now appreciate an overview of the three chapters in this book. In the opening chapter, "Sacramental Moments: Appreciative Awareness in the Iron Cage," Michael Cowan questions us on how responsive we are to the richness of mystery. The author first reviews the complex contexts of meaning in our world: "to live in culture, as creatures of meaning like ourselves always do, is to internalize deeply and unconsciously a disposition toward living."

We are anchored more deeply to our cultural and social world than we sometimes realize. Language is not the only symbol that we culturally share. As Cowan urgently reminds us, our moods and motivations also form part of this cultural disposition. Borrowing Max Weber's striking image of the "iron cage," the writer pointedly asks us how far our Western industrial society disposes us to superficial or even deformed meanings. By contrast, the appreciatively aware person continues to deepen his or her sense of mystery and the sacred.

Paul Philibert's chapter, "Readiness for Ritual: Psychological Aspects of Maturity in Christian Celebration," examines sacramental meaning and symbolic competency within the complementary context of the growing person. He contrasts the passive consumer of symbolic reality with those who experience a "symbolic hunger" for God's reality which is so much larger than our own. Philibert draws the lesson: "Liturgy can succeed only when the gospel stories are recognized as treasuries of life-giving preunderstandings which connect us in imagination and in desire with the promises of God's Kingdom preached by Jesus."

The heart of the problem is whether liturgical participants have a symbolic or a diabolic orientation. The symbolically oriented person finds the holy in the current ordinary situation. The diabolic orientation is fueled by a negative sense of obedience or fear. Celebrants and religious educators will be particularly sensitive to the pastoral implications of developmental factors that nourish this diabolic orientation.

Philibert helps the reader understand these developmental factors by reviewing Erik Erikson's stages of ritualization that reflect the stages of growth of the person: "Particular ritual qualities are acquired in distinct phases of development in the life cycle. Those qualities impact on key symbols of the Christian life." An important part of this ritual process is the community's ability to invite the growing person to "own" the shared values and vision of other members. The practical Christian test of ritualization is the symbolic competence which allows us to disown inadequate images of God and to adopt more mature ones. But the promotion of this symbolic competence will demand community leadership and action, and a theological language that resonates with the experiences of the growing religious person. Readiness for ritual, then, demands more awe and involvement, more vision and "re-vision" than we might first have believed.

The first two chapters provide a focus and understanding for Edward Kilmartin's insights in "Theology of the Sacraments: Toward a New Understanding of the Chief Rites of the Church of Jesus Christ." I can think of no one who might better introduce the reader into the rich heritage of sacramental history and, at the same time, outline new directions in rethinking our theology of sacraments. Kilmartin first sketches some of the key features of theological reflection on sacraments. He then discusses the connection between the human sciences and theology for the theory and *praxis* of sacrament. Finally, the author offers a new frame of reference for appreciating how we enter into God's self-communication. If readers are willing to stretch their minds, they will find Kilmartin's reflective essay a challenging invitation to review their own ideas on the meaning of sacrament.

In the first section of his chapter, Kilmartin shows how the question of sacrament in its historical perspective is part of a larger theological concern summed up in the query of Hugo of St. Victor: "What is the actual situation of humanity in the history of salvation?" Kilmartin points out how God's offer of self-communication is an essential part of the answer to that question in any historical epoch.

In the second section of his chapter, the author shows how the incarnational principle of God's action in the human situation calls for an interdisciplinary dialogue, which permits us to be sensitive to this sanctifying action in our world: "For the society in which we live provides us with a word, a timely word, which interprets these situations and so excludes or includes different possibilities of meaning or choice." In summarizing these first two sections, Kilmartin demonstrates how his concerns converge with those of Cowan and Philibert.

In the final section of his study, Kilmartin sounds the theme that he already suggested at the beginning of his work: "God's self-communication is realized historically through human communion, especially in liturgy." Retrieving the classical view of the sacramental character of all created reality, he carefully lays out the relations between God, Church, and the world. Within this perspective, "sacraments are special moments in the history of salvation, grounded on the Christ event." These moments contest our hopes limited by human achievement and urge us to look to the new possibilities which the Spirit actualizes in our own time.

Finally, when the sacraments are seen as the acts of the Church, the role of the ordained minister as representative of the community of Christ is put into proper perspective. The liturgy also enables intercommunication of believing Christians as they respond to God's self-communication. In these liturgical expressions of shared faith, the community becomes more open to the Spirit. These summary remarks do not do justice to the breadth of Kilmartin's thought but should suggest to readers that there are thundering pastoral questions behind the thoughtful statements of his work.

The future of sacramental participation and appropriation is being shaped now. We can learn from our past about our future. In the history of sacrament, it is fairly evident that when there has been a loss of symbolic thinking and action, it was accompanied by a change in sacramental questions. Symbolic thinking and action asks "why," a question of meaning, while the nonsymbolic mentality is only interested in "how" mystery is accomplished.

The contributors to this volume attempt to lead us back to the "why" of sacrament, a question which can only be understood within the complex contexts of our aging world and its growing people. These writers do not provide facile answers to the sacramental problems of our time but remind us of the familiar contours of our experience of God's communication and their implications for more honest sacrament. This is the magnificent capacity of sacrament: to make God's future real for us by the way it draws out both the Christian meaning of our past and its implications for our present. When sacrament is correctly understood and honestly symbolized, it always reflects the well-known urging of St. Augustine to his community in speaking of the sacrament of the Eucharist as the Body of Christ: "Be what you see—receive what you are."[2]

Footnotes

1. De Ghellinck et al., *Pour L'Histoire du Mot "Sacramentum"* (Louvain: Spicilegium Sacrum Lovaniense, 1924); J. Finkenzeller, *Die Lehre von den Sakramenten im allgemeinen. Von der Schrift bis zur Scholastik* (Freiburg: Herder, 1980).

2. St. Augustine, Sermon 272 (PL 38:1246).

1. SACRAMENTAL MOMENTS:
APPRECIATIVE AWARENESS IN THE IRON CAGE[1]

Michael A. Cowan

Resonances of Ultimacy

In sacred moments our depths resonate with the web of life; we touch on ultimate meanings and mysteries. The birth of a child and the death of a parent—intense moments of connection and loss—set us vibrating with the wonder and pain and beauty of our existence and dump the question of ultimate meaning squarely in our path. In loving acts and their aftermath and in moments of being forgotten, we are touched at the primal roots of human living.[2]

Such moments are not ours to command; they accost us, upsetting the everyday schedules which are our normal preoccupation. They flow over into everyday living, touching us deeply at least for a time. Sometimes our transformation is felt in a rush of hope which enlivens our loves and works. Or everyday life can be further emptied of meaning, and we sense the undertow of despair gathering force. What is the connection between life's sacred moments and a community's sacramental ones?

Sacramental moments within believing communities are the ritual occasions in which the religious faith of the members is celebrated and affirmed. In writing about religious symbols and practice Clifford Geertz has noted that

> It is in ritual that the conviction that religious conceptions are veridical and that religious directives are sound is somehow generated. It is in some sort of ceremonial form . . . that the moods and motivations which sacred symbols induce . . . and the general con-

ceptions of the order of existence which they formulate . . . meet
and reinforce one another. . . . It is, primarily at least, out of concrete acts of religious observance that religious conviction emerges
on the human plane.[3]

In concrete sacramental moments believing communities participate
in those occasions out of which, according to Geertz, religious convictions emerge concretely in human history.

It seems to me that if this analysis is correct, then sacramental
moments in Christian communities ought to trigger in us profound
resonances similar in kind if not always in intensity to the personal
experiences mentioned above in which our being is touched at its
core. Clearly for most persons in our time they simply do not. If
sacramental moments are doors to the sacred, they have surely
closed for many of us in Western culture today. If, as Gordon Kaufman has suggested, "God is the anchor-symbol for a whole way
of life and world view," then ritual moments must exist which per-
suade our hearts and minds of the rightness of such a world view.[4]
Many of us struggle to find such sacred moments today, especially
in formal religious worship.

Those who attempt to nurture the sacramental life of Christian
communities today do so in the belief that sacramental moments
among Christians are wellsprings for the ongoing creative transformation of the moods and motivations of persons and of the structures of society toward love. The introductory volume of this series
and the following volumes on particular sacraments have been created by interdisciplinary teams of theologians, social scientists, and
liturgists. Our hope and effort has been to encourage, support, and
challenge you in your efforts to bring communities together in
authentic sacramental moments. In inviting others to sacramental
experience today, we move against a historical tide which floods
everyday living in advanced industrial society with moods and motivations antithetical to the Christian disposition to love. The purpose of this volume and of the entire series is to sketch an image
of the tide against which we are swimming and to build a hope that
will sustain our efforts. My reflections throughout are centered on
human beings as "meaning-makers," and with this I will begin.

In the Light and Shadow of Meaning

The centrality of *meaning* in the unfolding of every person's life
and of our life together looms so large as I begin my reflection that
it is important to pause a moment and let such a massive presupposition be shared explicitly between us.

It seems to me undeniable that our lives originate in a dense web of relationships and unfold there from moment to moment until death. We are creatures rooted in the earth and yet restless there, searching for a sense of our connection with everyone and everything. We can also be quite individualistic in our orientation to life, oblivious to our interrelatedness within the world. We ask questions that other forms of life seemingly do not, and we love or hate each other because of our answers. If there is anything that we can say about human—as distinguished from animal, vegetable, or mineral—nature, it is that as humans we live, move, and have our becoming within the medium of meaning. How we feel about and act toward ourselves, each other, and our planet, depend upon what we can and cannot allow each to mean to us, because to be human is to be concerned primarily not with what something is in its physical makeup but with its significance for us.[5] And significance is always social in its origins; we are continually making it together.

I am looking at a drawing given to me recently by one of my daughters. It hangs in a place of honor near my writing table. As I take it in visually I remember and am drawn back into the feelings connected with the moments when she created it on the floor at my feet and proudly presented it to me. I also recall dozens of other moments in the unfolding of our connection as father and daughter from her beginning. This in turn evokes memories of my life before her—my own family, schools, friendships, marriage, work. As my heart and head touch these experiences again I find myself imagining future unfoldings of this web which is my life— the growth to maturity of my daughters, the deepening of family ties and the bonds of friendship, new work and people and places. Somehow this simple drawing, viewed in the present, calls up for me in a deep and touching way the organic unfolding of my existence out of a settled past and into possible futures.

As a matter of simple, physical fact, the object on the wall in front of me is a piece of white paper roughly five inches high and eight inches wide with thirteen "squiggly" lines of various colors clustered unevenly on its surface. But to be human is to operate constantly out of a deep but usually taken-for-granted sense not of what things are, but of what they mean to us. In fact quite a lot of discipline is involved in learning to go "back to the things themselves:" to concern ourselves with such elements as bare forms, textures, colors.[6] Human beings are born into worlds of symbolic meaning, participate in their ongoing transformation, and die amidst them. The significance that we attribute to our living and dying massively shapes their qualities and effects.

A person perceiving an object as a chair and sitting on it; an infant learning to recognize and name Mama; a revolutionary organizing a network for the violent overthrow of an oppressive political regime in the name of social justice; a civil servant projecting unemployment curves, and a community of persons gathered around a table to break bread and share a cup and identify their experience in the present with the life of Jesus: these are all human beings engaged in what we are fundamentally about, composing present moments of experience in the light and shadow of meanings inherited from culture.

Inheriting a World

How does culture provide us a heritage of meanings which offers coherence and purpose in our lives? In the analysis of Clifford Geertz, which I will follow here, *culture* designates

> An historically transmitted pattern of meanings embodied in symbols, a system of inherited conceptions expressed in symbolic forms by means of which persons communicate, perpetuate and develop their knowledge about and attitudes toward life.[7]

It is an exploration of this understanding of culture which will generate light to guide us in exploring the problem of experiencing sacramentally today.

A culture's meanings are carried and transmitted in its *symbols.* Symbols are sources of information, filters or templates which give our experiencing particular forms. These sources of information are not contained in our genes; they initially reside outside our bodies in the world of shared meanings which is a culture. As we become absorbed in a particular symbolic world, or culture, we learn to experience in a specific, culturally informed way.[8]

A potent and pervasive example of the symbolic guiding of our way of experiencing is to be found in the role of language in our lives. The words of a language are symbols as defined above. The following account illustrates the symbolic shaping of experience via language.

> In Maidu, an American Indian language of Northern California, only three words are available to describe the color spectrum. They divide the spectrum as follows . . .
>
> | *lak* | *tit* | *tulak* |
> |---|---|---|
> | (red) | (green-blue) | (yellow-orange-brown) |
>
> While human beings are capable of making 7,500,000 different color

distinctions in the visible color spectrum, the people who are native speakers of Maidu habitually group their experience into three categories supplied by their language. These three Maidu color terms cover the same range of real-world sensations which the eight (basic) color terms of English do. Here the point is that a person who speaks Maidu is characteristically conscious of only three categories of color experience while the English speaker has more categories and, therefore, more habitual perceptual distinctions. This means, that, while English speakers will describe their experience of two objects as different (say, a yellow book and an orange book), speakers of Maidu will typically describe their experience of the identical real-world situation as being the same (two *tulak* books).[9]

In this example the number of typical color distinctions in two languages affects the experiencing of their native speakers in a profound and simple way: with the same two objects in front of them, an English speaker sees one yellow book and one orange book; a Maidu speaker sees two *tulak* books.

Every word in our language and the particular structures of grammar, syntax, and genre by which we combine smaller meaning units into larger ones have constant effects on our experiencing that are like the effects of the color words on English and Maidu experiencing. Our language never merely describes "the facts" of our world, but functions like a lens to influence what stands out in our experience and what remains in the background. When, for example, a person in our culture is designated a "man" he learns to see himself and others learn to see him in a particular way. It has been one of the gifts of the women's movement to raise our awareness about how many of our traditional connotations regarding masculinity are destructive to men and women alike. To be a creature of language, and therefore of symbol, is to learn to experience reality in the symbolic forms mediated by a culture.

The pattern of inherited meanings which constitutes a culture always carries an understanding of how things are in the universe, of what the structure of reality is. This picture of the way things are is the *world view* of a culture.[10] It may be a highly complex and analytical account of various levels of reality and their interrelationship, complete with empirical evidence to support that analysis. Or it may be a rough-and-ready division of reality into matter and spirit, arrived at intuitively or by some historic revelation. Our world view as members of a culture is for the most part taken for granted by us. It will ordinarily be called to our explicit attention only if it fails to work in some practical way or if our work involves direct reflection on the structure of reality or some particular aspects of it.[11] In learning a language and the other forms of lifelong socialization, we unconsciously absorb a sense of the character of reality which will serve as a presupposed metaphysics or map of reality from our births to our deaths.

Our inherited cultural conceptions also always carry with them a sense of how our life ought to be lived, of the human style of life appropriate to a reality structured according to the world view or implicit metaphysics just mentioned. This appropriate way of life is the *ethos* of a culture.[12] Our word ethic comes from the same root. An ethos may dictate a highly detailed set of steps for the composition of our days or merely offer general guidelines to be observed in pursuing our personal interests. As we become enculturated as a member of our group, we internalize a sense of how our lives ought to be lived if we are to be valued by the other participants in our cultural world. This sense of a proper style of living will serve as a largely unconscious personal and social ethic for the conduct of our lives.

The world view and ethos of a culture are correlated. Our image of the way things are supports our style of living by showing its rationality, the goodness of its fit with actual conditions. Our style of life supports our implicit metaphysics by showing how well-suited reality is to the way of living we have created. In the words of Geertz:

> A group's ethos is rendered intellectually reasonable by being shown to represent a way of life ideally adapted to the actual state of affairs the world view describes, while the world view is rendered emotionally convincing by being presented as an image of an actual state of affairs peculiarly well-arranged to accommodate such a way of life.[13]

By living in and absorbing the symbolic code by means of which our people organize their world, we become and remain one of them. We also soak up, as if by osmosis, a view of how reality works and a correlative sense of the good life within such a reality. These will serve us as lifelong pathways for orienting our existence from day to day.[14]

To live in culture, as creatures of meaning like ourselves always do, is to internalize deeply and unconsciously a disposition toward living. By a disposition I mean a particular set of *moods* and *motivations* that gives a unique tone and structure to a people's experience. When we speak of the reserve of the British or the discipline of the Germans or the pragmatism of Americans we are trying, however clumsily and partially, to name something about the "deep stories" that persons are born into and live out of as members of various cultures.[15] What are these moods and motivations, and how are they played out in our lives together?

By *moods* I mean underlying feelings about life that pervade the experience of people in a culture.[16] This does not mean that every person in the group will always feel this way, but that there is a tendency within the group to share a particular deep feeling response toward their existence. When we speak of American optimism we know very well that not every American is always optimistic, and yet this mood has seemed to many an apt description of an important feeling-tone in the American experience. The same can be said of Greek zestfulness and Gaelic romanticism: they describe not a way that everyone in those cultural groups always feels, but a tendency within the groups to share a particular feeling response to life.

By *motivations* I mean shared tendencies to behave in particular ways.[17] We Americans, for example, tend toward activism in our motives. We want to "do something," to "make something happen," to "get on with it," or to "get it over with." Once again, this does not mean that all Americans are activists but that a tendency toward activism is a deep inclination within the American experience.

To be a member of a particular culture is to share not only common symbols, especially the same language, and therefore a common world view and ethos, but also a common disposition of moods and motivations. The extraordinary power of culture resides partly in the fact that we ordinarily take its most basic assumptions and guidelines for living entirely for granted. The moods and motives of a cultural world become for us the "natural" way of being human.[18] It is only when they fail to work or are subject to radical challenge that we step back from our taken-for-granted symbolic worlds with their accompanying moods and motives and become aware of alternative possibilities for being human. For example, the bitter experience of Vietnam forced many Americans to a deep and painful questioning of our optimistic moods and "can-do" motivations (although regretfully one still hears that America's mistake in that case was failing "to turn North Vietnam into a parking lot").

We exist in the pathways of culture like fish in water. The pervasiveness of our enculturation is matched only by the extent of our lack of awareness of the degree to which we are enculturated. Like the fish we ordinarily do not experience ourselves as wet. The pattern of meanings of our *culture* is embodied in *symbols.* To live within those symbolic meanings is to absorb a *world view* and an *ethos.* At the heart of a people's cultural way of life are shared dispositions, common *moods* and *motivations,* which embody the particular spirit of a people. As human beings the question is not whether we operate symbolically within a particular world view and ethos, but rather what symbolic universe we inhabit. The issue is not whether our shared symbolic world disposes us toward a particular constellation of moods and motivations, but rather to what set of emotional and behavioral dispositions we are inclined.

So when human beings gather for liturgical celebration, we come from having spent our lives in a particular symbolic world, a culture, with its accompanying moods and motivations. We can experience ritual moments only from within the world of meaning within which we live. We return to a social world oriented to those common meanings. What that world of meaning is and how it disposes people within it toward life is of enormous import for a community's celebration of sacred moments:

> The dispositions which religious rituals induce have their most important impact—from a human point of view—outside the boundaries of the ritual itself as they reflect back to color the individual's conception of the established world of bare fact. The peculiar tone [of various religious rituals] pervades areas of people's lives far beyond the immediately religious, impressing upon them a distinctive style in the sense both of a dominant mood and a characteristic movement.[19]

In this quotation Geertz describes the profound impact of religious rituals in preindustrial cultures. Do sacramental occasions in our contemporary industrialized society have a chance at profound effects of their own?

In religious rituals the events of our everyday lives can be placed in an ultimate context or left outside the door as we enter for a time into a separate enclave of meaning.[20] In sacramental moments our daily experience can be brought into contrast and creative tension with sacred stories or left in a vacuum as regards the ultimate. When the symbolic worlds of everyday life and of religious ritual are too far removed from each other, a split in the consciousness of believers is the inevitable result. We find it more and more difficult to experience sacramental occasions as pervasively transforming our everyday lives. Religious significance, if it survives at all, is relegated to private moments in our lives. The publicness of the sacred vanishes.

Our collective symbolic split has emerged largely because whereas sacred symbols in Western culture have traditionally invoked an otherworldy dimension of reality, the world view of everyday life in Western culture is thoroughly natural in its orientation. From the very insides of matter to the farthest cosmic reaches we know our world as an extraordinarily complex and integrated whole. In fact our finest scientific minds have for some time now accustomed us to the idea that the same physical laws describe both the mechanics of quanta and the unfolding of galaxies. In the everyday world view of contemporary people in Western culture there is no "other world."

When modern persons transcend life's surface and experience resonances of ultimacy, our routes are not out of life but into its depths. Sacramental experiences, shrouded in the language and invoking the image of two worlds, one natural and one supernatural, do not locate the everyday experience of most contemporary Western persons on meaningful ultimate horizons, and therefore cannot be doorways to authentic religious experience for them. For such persons transcendence has profound meaning in connection with our common human experience of the limits and the depths, the complexity and incomprehensibility of our one world; it is virtually emptied of meaning when it invokes another—let alone a wholly other—world. For most of us today supernatural religious images bar the doors to the sacred, distancing us from a profound sense of the mystery immanent in the web of our lives.[21] The challenge we face in seeking out the religious depths of our experience is not the recovery of another and sacred world, but the sacralizing of the one world out of which our existence emerges.

In his retrospective and prospective analysis of sacramental theology in this volume, Edward Kilmartin offers an extremely cogent analysis which sheds light on how a supernatural orientation to the sacraments evolved. He also offers a strong case for the importance of revising that stance in the direction of sacraments understood as the self-expression of the Church in the world. From this perspective the sacramentalizing of various moments of human life does not reside in ritual forms but rather in a liturgical community's symbolic expression of sacred presence in the world. And the core of such expression is communicative action within a social group and from that group to the world beyond it.

How a people's everyday world view and ethos dispose them toward life, what moods and motivations are their cultural heritage, is of enormous import for a community's celebration of life's sacredness. A community's sacramental moments may have similar import in the transformation of its people's moods and motivations for everday life in their culture. In fact the ritual transformation of our deeply held dispositions in living—our collective moods and motivations—is the most powerful contribution to the concrete history of human life in the world which can occur in a community's sacramental moments.

Life in the Iron Cage

Let us take the notion that culture means not only common symbols but also shared tendencies in moods and motivations and see whether we can discern a pattern in the lives of American people today. It must be noted at this point that cultural pluralism and economic differences within American society make it quite difficult to generalize about such things. As a Western nation the United States has a special cultural heritage that it holds in common with European peoples, but African, Hispanic, and Asian cultures also have deep and vital connections to the American cultural experience, affecting it in increasingly important ways.

Three characteristics of contemporary American society can help us seek out our shared cultural moods and motivations. First, in keeping with the dominant pattern among Western nations, we are an advanced industrial society. Second, the underlying tendency of the American style of living is to pursue our ends actively using our planet and other persons as means. Third, we are profoundly individualistic in our styles of life.

An advanced industrial society is one which has undergone two important transformations in its basic economic structure.[22] The first of these, which initially occurred in England between 1750 and 1850, is a shift of the majority of workers from agriculture to industry. The second, which continues today, is the shift of a significant number of workers from industrial to service occupations. An advanced industrial society is one in which a large proportion of the labor force is employed in such areas as health, education, government, and retailing. Such a society requires an incredibly intricate network of production and distribution, transportation, communication, government and legal systems.

The social organization that makes the evolution of such a complex and interdependent society possible is the bureaucracy.[23] As regards the nature and purpose of the bureaucracy, Max Weber has written:

> The decisive reason for the advance of bureaucratic organization has always been its purely technical superiority over any other form of organization. The fully developed bureaucratic mechanism compares with other organizations exactly as does the machine with the non-mechanical modes of production.
>
> Precision, speed, unambiguity, knowledge of the files, discretion, unity, strict subordination, reduction of friction and of material and personal costs—these are raised to the optimum point in the strictly bureaucratic administration.[24]

The ordering of resources for maximum efficiency in the pursuit of goals is the characteristic of bureaucratic social organization.

The hallmark of a well-functioning bureaucracy is rationality in the pursuit of goals. Following the impulses of the moment or worrying too much about the ultimate implications of a course of action threaten the order necessary to this form of social organization, and such activities will tend to be squeezed out over time in the bureaucracy's pursuit of rational courses of action.

Those who survive in a bureaucratic world, and today this means almost everyone in Western culture, are those who learn the system's rules and live within them. We must do what is required whether or not it feels good at the moment and must not challenge too strongly the system's right to make certain demands even if they conflict with our ultimate values. For example, as bona fide citizens of the United States we may have and express any feelings we wish about our country's nuclear arms policy. This policy may fit or clash with our ultimate values and beliefs. But should a large number of us refuse to pay a portion of our income taxes as a protest against those policies, then we must face legal consequences or the bureaucracy loses its ability to function effectively on this issue. As employees of a large corporation we have a perfect right to our "private" feelings and values, but should these lead us to challenge too drastically the way our firm does business we will likely jeopardize our employment. As a woman within the Catholic Church, one's opinions and feelings about the ordination of persons of her sex to the priesthood are her prerogative, but should she take this issue too dramatically into her own hands her formal membership in the Church will be threatened.

The underpinning of an advanced industrial society is an interlocked network of large bureaucratically and hierarchically organized structures. Such structures are to be found in all the major sectors of our society. These large bureaucratic structures are not independent of each other but form a massively interlocked foundation on which our social order rests.[25] The spirit of the bureaucracy, as embodied in rational planning, role hierarchies, and discipline in the pursuit of goals, pervades every aspect of our lives as American people.

Weber had a haunting image of what Western societies were becoming, an iron cage in which increasingly rational or bureaucratic social organization would gradually crush our capacity to be attuned to the magic and mystery of our world.[26] In reflection on the bureaucratization of the Western world Weber wrote:

> The fate of our times is characterized by rationalization and intellectualization and, above all, by the "disenchantment of the world." Precisely the ultimate and most sublime values have retreated from public life either into the transcendental realm of mystic life or into the brotherliness of direct and personal human relations. It is not accidental that our greatest art is intimate and not monumental, and that today only within the smallest and most intimate circles . . . that something is pulsating that corresponds to the prophetic *pneuma*, which in former times swept through the great communities like a firebrand, welding them together.[27]

The great challenge for liturgical celebration in our time is to refuse to be swept into the rational/instrumental mainstream of Western cultural life, or relegated to nurturing only private or small group forms of religious experience. Rather, a community's sacramental moments must seek ways of sustaining and deepening a sense of the sacredness of life in the world for all of its people.

Weber's fear was that we would find ourselves living together in an efficient but grey world, longing for color but unable to find it in our iron cage of efficiency. In attempting to describe the roots of our loss of the sense of realities beyond our control, Weber wrote that the rationalization and bureaucratization of modern life is based on the belief that

> There are no mysterious incalculable forces that come into play, but rather that one can, in principle, master all things by calculation. This means that the world is disenchanted. One need no longer have recourse to magical means in order to master or implore the spirits, as did the savage for whom such mysterious powers existed. Technical means and calculations provide the service. This is above all what these developments mean.[28]

Our problems and challenges are subject to rational problem-solving and solution: we can master all things by calculation. There is no mystery which cannot be managed. The bureaucracy is the social form which exemplifies this orientation, the social embodiment of the iron cage.

For many contemporary Americans Weber's prophecy has been fulfilled. Assembly lines, government bureaucracies, corporate ladders, welfare and educational systems, and overly institutionalized religious organizations are the bars of our cage. They are progressively choking off our capacity to experience the wonder of the gift of life, disposing us instead to see our existence as something to be survived or coped with or dominated. Ironically it is often said that the very social invention which allowed for the remarkable socioeconomic development of the West—the bureaucracy—is now a major source of the crises and impasses of Western democracies.[29]

Of course our present difficulties have to do not only with certain characteristics of the bureaucracy as a social form but also with the ends toward which bureaucracies are oriented. The accumulation of wealth is one sort of bureaucratic agenda, the provision of adequate education or medical care another. The awareness of bureaucracies as systems having profound effects on all our lives and the issue of how such systems can and ought to be transformed raise anew the question of emphasizing personal versus corporate responsibility for Christian existence in the world.

During Christian history since the Enlightenment, individuals have been called to *metanoia*, not relational webs or systems. This stress on individual morality and salvation is heightened within the profoundly individualistic world view and ethos characteristic of American culture. In *Habits of the Heart* Robert Bellah and his associates offer a penetrating analysis of patterns of individualism and commitment in American life.[30] Their sobering conclusion is that our culture has extended individualism nearly to the breaking point. Our world view and ethos now reflect a kind of "ontological individualism" in which the individual has a kind of primary reality, while society is understood as derived from the primary reality of individuals.

In a thoroughly relational world the need to transform systems cannot be ignored by those seeking the embodiment of Christian values in history. This transformation requires different sensitivities, strategies, skills, and commitments than did the call to individual change. It is a different thing to organize a minority community into an effective political and economic force than to encourage members of a parish toward personal holiness.

Again the one versus two-world issue arises. Our religious traditions in the West, following the natural/supernatural splitting of worlds, have tended to understand and therefore encourage disengagement from the processes and events of the natural ("profane") world as the path toward salvation. Involvement in the transformation of "natural" realities such as political and economic systems tends to be devalued in a two-world view; we are urged to set our sights and orient our lives to the "really real" other world. In a one-world view a Christian stance in life pressures us toward deeper and broader commitments in the concrete historical web within which our lives are pitched. Not distance but engagement becomes the watchword of Christian presence in the one-world view.

Weber's iron cage is an image applicable to any Western advanced industrial society. Sociologist Talcott Parsons offers a description of what he sees as the underlying spirit or disposition of the American version of advanced industrial society in the label "instrumental activism."[31] An instrumental stance is a tendency to see things and people as means to one's ends. An activistic orientation is a tendency to exercise initiative in pursuing one's goals. Two people strolling in the woods come upon a rushing river. An appreciative or receptive response might involve a reflection on the beauty and power of nature; an instrumentally activistic response might involve estimating how much hydroelectric power could be generated if a dam were erected at such-and-such a location on the river.[32]

The spirit of individualistic instrumental activism is the disposition that underlies much that the United States has accomplished. Our standard of living and technological accomplishments are among its fruits. But this stance has its daemonic side as well. The near destruction of native American culture, the air in the northwestern corner of Indiana, and the exploitation of Latin American people and resources are also among its fruits.

The descriptions of our world as an iron cage and of our lives as individualistic exercises in instrumental activism point to the underlying moods and motivations of everyday life in the contemporary American version of advanced industrial society. As American people an individualistic and instrumentally active way of being in the world is in our bones. This stance points to the meanings, moods, and motivations which we bring with us today to the experience of sacramental moments. It is this individualistic instrumental disposition toward living that must be transformed if ritual moments are to flow into everyday life in a way that makes large differences. Let us look more deeply at dispositions as meaning-orientations for human lives.

Four Dispositions

The dominant moods and motivations of our everyday lives, as exemplified in addiction to individual achievement or rage at being denied fair opportunity, are those of people who take for granted the active pursuit of our individual goals and the appropriateness of using our planet and other people as means. One troubling instance of this disposition is the incredible amount of damage to family life which is routinely accepted by persons in our culture intent on the pursuit of success in their occupations. On a larger scale we are faced continually with the possible—some would say inevitable—destruction of human life in our persistent inclination toward the employment of unilateral power in pursuing "*the* national interest" within the web of nations.[33]

How we respond to other persons, events, and things depends upon what we can and cannot allow them to mean to us. As noted in part two of this chapter, to be human is to be concerned not primarily with what things are but what they mean. In my dealings with you it is not my intentions and behaviors in themselves that will elicit your reaction, but your reading of their meaning. That reading in turn emerges from the meanings of the millions of moments in your life which preceded it. Contemporary research on human development over the course of life has pointed to predictable stages in this process of making meaning.[34] As human beings we can move throughout our lives toward greater levels of complexity and integration in our ways of construing the meanings which guide our actions. The chapter in this volume on symbolic competence by Paul Philibert offers an informative picture of stages in the ritualization of human experience based on Erik Erikson's pioneer work. In Philibert's treatment of symbolic versus diabolic meaning-making and of stages in the development of God-imagery over our lifetimes, an important message regarding the making of meaning emerges: as developing persons we do not employ a static way of making sense of ultimate realities in our world. Rather, the meaning of the sacred and its effects in our lives can and do undergo profound transformation over the entire life cycle. Human beings take their cultures' meanings and transform them creatively.

In order to understand the effects of something or someone in your life, I must hear the story of that presence as experienced by you. This principle of the centrality of meaning in human action is summarized in the classic dictum of sociologist W. I. Thomas: "If [people] define situations as real, they are real in their consequences."[35]

If the effects in my life of other persons, events, and things depend on my reading of their meaning, then what sorts of dispositions toward my world are possible for me? I would like to describe briefly four orientations to life from the standpoint of the meaning that we allow our world to have for us in each of them. I will call the orientations *transferential, contemporaneous, instrumental,* and *receptive.*

Transferential describes relationships in which my reaction to my world is so dominated by the effects of persons and events from my past, especially authority figures from childhood, that what this moment means to me has little relationship to what is actually occurring here and now.[36] Such relating involves unconsciously misidentifying events now with those which loomed large in my history. We form relationships in which "we must grope around for each other through a dense thicket of absent others. We cannot see each other plain. A horrible kind of predestination hovers over each new attachment we form."[37] In transferential relating my past, rather than the present as it is, overdetermines what this moment of my life can and cannot mean.

Contemporaneous names a type of relationship in which the meaning that this moment has for me is not dominated by my history but is rooted primarily in what is transpiring in the present. In this second orientation novel possibilities of meaning are not automatically crushed under the weight of the past. I allow the moment its uniqueness. In contemporaneous relating present events, rather than those of the past, principally determine what this presence in my life can mean.

Instrumental describes a mode of relating in which what the moment means to me is determined by the ways that it fits or fails to fit into my agenda, my life's hopes and goals. In the simplest terms this is an orientation to relationship in which persons, events, and things are primarily a means to my ends. The hallmark of a culture with strong tendencies in the direction of individualistic instrumental activism is that relations between people and our actions toward our planet are tinctured by utility, that we routinely see our physical and social worlds as tools. In instrumental relating my agenda, rather than yours or ours or life's, determines what events in my life can and cannot mean.

Receptive names a pattern of relationship in which what my world means to me is not dominated by my history or what I wish to accomplish at the moment. I seek to receive respectfully the offering of the present. In our instrumentalist culture receptive is too easily translated as passive; a more appropriate synonym would be appreciative. In receptive relating larger meanings and possibilities for life than mine alone determine what the present can mean.

Each unfolding moment of our lives is likely to be received with a mixture of the four attitudes just discussed. Our reaction will be affected by the important relationships in our histories and is, therefore, partially transferential. It will take some account of the actual presence of events here and now and is therefore partially contemporaneous. Its meaning to us will be shaped by the ways that it affects our plans and hopes and therefore will be in part instrumental. It will involve some recognition of otherness, however minimal, and is therefore to some degree receptive. The question is this: what are the proportions of each orientation in our typical collective cultural disposition toward otherness?

Men in our rationally instrumentally activistic culture tend toward an instrumental/transferential style of relating. The instrumentalness of our orientation is no doubt shaped by the cultural fact that it has until quite recently been our primary task to go into the economic arena, which is organized along rational and instrumental lines, in order to provide for the material well-being of our families. The transferential side of our orientation originates from unresolved issues within our families of origin which continue to be played out in adult life. Issues of being emotionally "owned" or dominated seem particularly salient for men in our culture.[38]

It seems to me that women in our culture are disposed toward a receptive/transferential style of being in relationships. The roots of the transferential side are also to be found in unresolved family-of-origin experiences being continued in the present. Issues of being forgotten, or of not mattering, seem particularly powerful for women in our culture. The receptive emphasis is no doubt shaped by the cultural fact that until recently women have been charged with primary responsibility for the physical and emotional well-being of their families.[39]

The cost of this psychosocial differentiation by sex or sex-role stereotyping, which is correlated with a historical socioeconomic division of labor according to sex, is that all too often we find men in our culture so absorbed in pursuing work-related responsibilities and goals that their sensitivity to the full range of their own needs and feelings and those of spouses, children, and friends is seriously underdeveloped. Enter the Marlboro Man. We also find women struggling to claim their right to competence and achievement outside the home without sacrificing their relational sensitivities and commitments. This is a complex and often heart-rending task which all too frequently ends in demoralized withdrawal from the economic arena or the emergence of the "Marlboro Woman."[40]

Our iron cage and the hectic individualistic achieving that we are driven to in order to keep some life and meaning within it, incline us strongly toward a stance of responding to other people and our planet as things to be used in the pursuit of individual achievement. To be a contemporary male American is to live out of such a disposition almost automatically. The alienation and despair that many of us routinely feel in work, family, and personal life in our culture is correlated with the moods and motives of individualistic instrumental activism into which we are socialized from birth. These are the dispositions toward living—the underlying moods and motivations—which sacramental experiences in Christian communities within American culture today must touch and transform if our everyday moods and motivations are to be profoundly challenged by a sacred story with the ultimate in noninstrumental stances—love—at its center.

The Moods and Motives of Appreciative Awareness

A capacity for sacramental experiences, events which orient us toward the sacred, the ultimate, the mysterious in living, is too often lost in instrumentally active lives played out in the iron cage. A sense of wonder is not easily nurtured in a world preoccupied with rational, technological, and material goal-seeking by individuals. Our shared disposition to individualistic instrumental activism blocks our access to the sacred.

"Appreciative awareness" is theologian Bernard Meland's description of a disposition toward living that counterbalances our collective tendency toward instrumental activism.[41] Appreciative awareness of a person, place, thing, symbol, or of our universe itself

takes as its starting point the mystery of what is given in existence. . . . This means the full richness of the concrete event with all of its possibilities and relations, imagined or perceived. The thing, in and of itself, apart from any instrumental or functional purpose, any rational or moral preference, becomes the object of inquiry. Thus receptiveness to the datum envisaged becomes the initial conscious response. The datum with all its mystery is received in wonder. The objective event is enabled to declare itself.[42]

While the starting point of the instrumentally active awareness is, as noted above, that all things can be mastered by calculation, the starting point of appreciative awareness is a receptive response to our world and an apprehending of its qualities for their own sake. In such moments persons and things and events speak to us partly on their own terms rather than being totally fit into niches predetermined by our histories and agendas. Let us look briefly at the appreciative awareness of others, of culture, and of nature.

When we open ourselves to hearing stories of others' lives, we are disposing ourselves toward appreciative awareness. In the language of the previous section of this chapter, we are adopting a receptive and contemporaneous stance toward the other person, neither seeing them chiefly as means to our ends nor distorting who they are because of our history. The significance of our appreciative awareness of each other and of our failures in that regard has been expressed powerfully by Martin Buber:

> The basis of our lives together is twofold, and it is one—the wish of all of us to be confirmed by others as what we are, even as what we can become; and the innate capacity in us to confirm each other in this way. That this capacity lies so immeasurably fallow constitutes the real weakness and questionableness of the human race: actual humanity exists only where this capacity unfolds.[43]

In developing the discipline and tenderness and resilience of spirit to receive each other as we are, the spirit in us is enlivened and deepened.

This same appreciative stance can also characterize our way of taking account of the symbols and meanings of our own and other cultures. While maintaining an open and growing appreciation of the symbols of our own culture is difficult enough, the appreciative awareness of other cultures with their accompanying moods and motivations is perhaps the most important challenge for us as contemporary inhabitants of a global village.[44] A beautiful statement of how we can begin is found in the words of John V. Taylor:

> Our first task in approaching another people, another culture, another religion, is to take off our shoes, for the place we are approaching is holy. Else we may find ourselves treading on others' dreams. More serious, still, we may forget that God was there before our arrival.[45]

In taking off our shoes as we approach others' holy places, the spirit in us transcends the vision—the world view and ethos—of its culture-of-origin and begins to internalize the breadth and depths of human experience in the world.

The power of an appreciative awareness of nature to bring us into contact with ultimate realities shines out in the poetry of Wordsworth, as in these lines:

> For I have learned
> To look on nature, not as in the hour
> Of thoughtless youth; but hearing often times
> The still, sad music of humanity,
> Nor harsh nor grating, though of ample power
> To chasten and subdue. And I have felt
> A presence that disturbs me with the joy
> Of elevated thoughts; a sense sublime
> Of something far more deeply interfused,
> Whose dwelling is the light of setting suns,
> And the round ocean and the living air,
> And the blue sky, and in the mind of man:
> A motion and a spirit, that impels
> All thinking things, all objects of all thought,
> And rolls through all things. Therefore am I still
> A lover of the meadows and the woods,
> And mountains; and of all that we behold
> From this green earth. . . .[46]

In the quiet and simple language of Irish poet Patrick Kavanagh a similar image is evoked:

> Child there is light somewhere
> Under a star,
> Sometime it will be for you
> A window that looks
> Inward to God.[47]

In appreciative encounters with nature, the spirit in us catches glimpses of its origin and destiny.

Appreciative awareness will sometimes leave one with an incredible sense of life as an unearned gift and sometimes with a terrifying sense of the irreducible ambiguity of our existence.[48] In either case authentic moments of appreciative awareness add depth and intensity to our world because something or someone that was outside our experience has now become woven into its fabric. The stature of our spirit has become enlarged.

In moments of appreciative awareness we sense, however dimly, the ongoing emergence of life from the web of relationships which is life's womb.

> It is by apprehending the signs and intimations which are constantly occurring within this complexity that one comes upon the truth of any situation. These signs and intimations are always of a transitive and relational character. They are discerned, not in the noting or measuring of fixed facts, but in the attending to the process wherein the facts are moving toward new facts or toward a new status by reason of other facts or other circumstances. They are discerned, not in the single entity, but in the pattern of relationships which forms the depth of every event or experience, and thus contains the resources which point up the tendencies and possibilities in any situation.[49]

The *mood* which accompanies such an awareness of life is reverence, sometimes pained, sometimes joyful. The *motivation* that it spawns is devotion to the fragile and ambiguous beauty of life.

The lives of persons in our society, which is so thoroughly committed to the individualistic instrumental activism described above, are desperately in need of social and communal structures that nurture a reverent devotion to life. It seems to me that these moods and motives are precisely what ritual or sacramental experiences in Christian communities can both tap and nurture.

> The meaning of the Christian faith is in this venture of hope and determination that what has begun in creation, the turning of sheer process in a sensitive direction, in the emergence of a child or a tender shoot, or in the fruition of the human spirit, shall be carried to an ultimate destiny.[50]

In the central Christian sacramental moment, for example, a community of persons gathers around a table to break bread and share a cup and identify their experience in the present with the life of Jesus. Contemporary eucharistic theology would suggest that in breaking the bread we acknowledge that we are one body; in sharing the cup we pledge ourselves to ever deeper engagement in shared living.[51]

At their best, sacramental moments in Christian community reorient us to the sacredness of the communal or relational character of our living and to a religious appreciation of life emerging continuously in the web of relations among persons, places, symbols, and things which is our world. But those who attempt to nurture sacramental moments in Christian communities should be aware that the tide of everyday living in American advanced industrial society shapes the experience of all of us in precisely the opposite direction, that is, toward a life of individual instrumental activism in the deepening dusk of the iron cage.

If bureaucratic organizations are the social birthplace of the moods and motivations of instrumental activism, believing communities must be wombs which nurture a collective disposition of appreciative awareness:

> The fruition of the human spirit, and the completion of the Creator's intent in our lives, demands the development of an appreciative consciousness in people, in which the affections of men and women, their hungers and longings shall express the spiritual intent of their natures. Blessed are they who hunger and thirst after righteousness, for they shall be filled. This promise can be fulfilled only as the appreciation of spirit is awakened and the processes creative of good are made ample and operative in the institutions that nurture our lives.[52]

When we are appreciatively disposed, the deep feelings flowing out of our existence in the world—our moods—and our tendencies toward action in the world—our motivations—are those of persons who receive reverently other individuals, cultures, and the planet itself. We allow the "other" its uniqueness and refrain from greeting it merely as a means to our ends, whether personal, political, or religious.

In an irreducibly pluralistic age equipped with life or death-giving technology, a collective appreciative disposition holds the only hope for future generations to stand on our shoulders and move back our horizons of meaning. The sacramental moments of Christian communities can be critical centers of awareness and energy for tincturing our collective instrumental activism with an appreciation of the sacredness and the mystery of our universe and of the fragile human experiment which is emerging within its womb.

Footnotes

1. The social and cultural analysis contained in this essay was nurtured in hours of dialogue with my friend and colleague Richard P. Albares of St. John's University, Collegeville, Minnesota. A sense of the profound sociality of human existence in the world has been his gift to me.

2. For my understanding of love and loss as the two sources of energy for a human life, I am indebted to Daniel F. Carle.

3. This quotation is drawn from an essay entitled "Religion as a cultural system" by Clifford Geertz published in his collection of essays, *The Interpretation of Cultures* (New York: Basic Books, 1973) 112.

4. Gordon Kaufman, *The Problem of God* (Cambridge, Mass.: Harvard, 1972) 100.

5. The orientation to meaning which guides the writing of this essay follows the interpretation of Susanne K. Langer in *Philosophy in a New Key* (Cambridge, Mass.: Harvard, 1957) chap. 2-5.

I am also heavily indebted, as was Langer, to the understanding of symbolic perception which is one aspect of Alfred Whitehead's theory of experience.

A readable account of this doctrine of perception can be found in A. N. White-head, *Symbolism: Its Meaning and Effect* (New York: Macmillan, 1972). A technical and scholarly analysis of the evolution of Whitehead's perceptual theory can be found in Paul F. Schmidt, *Perception and Cosmology in Whitehead's Philosophy* (New Brunswick, N.J.: Rutgers, 1967).

The theological import of meaning's centrality in human existence is clearly and simply examined in Tad Guzie, *Jesus and the Eucharist* (New York: Paulist Press, 1974) chap. 2, "Two Questions about Reality" and passim.

6. This is Edmund Husserl's dictum for phenomenological method in philosophy. See, for example, Edmund Husserl, *The Idea of Phenomenology* (The Hague: Martinus Nijhoff, 1973) 1.

7. Geertz, *The Interpretation of Cultures* 89.

Geertz's approach to the understanding of culture is *semiotic*, i.e., concentrates on symbolic meaning as the central perspective for understanding how culture functions. He follows the definition of symbol proposed by Langer (see note 5 above).

The essay cited here and in note 3 above provides a framework which I will draw on extensively in this section of the essay.

8. *Ibid.* 92-94.

9. R. Bandler and J. Grinder, *The Structure of Magic* (Palo Alto, Calif.: Science and Behavior Books, 1975) 1:10-11.

For a more technical treatment of the perceptual filtering function of language see H. Hoijer, "The Sapir-Whorf Hypothesis" in L. Samovar and R. Porter, *Intercultural Communication* (Belmont, Calif.: Wadsworth, 1972) 150-158.

10. Geertz, *The Interpretation of Cultures* 89-90.

11. See, for example, Martin Heidegger's insightful analysis of what happens when our cultural "equipment" fails to function as it should in Martin Heidegger, *Being and Time*, trans. John Macquarrie and Edward Robinson (New York: Harper & Row, 1962) especially Part I, section 3, 102-107.

12. Geertz, *The Interpretation of Cultures* 89-90.

13. *Ibid.* 89-90.

14. Cf. Heidegger's analysis of being-in-the-world as involvement in an interconnected referential structure in *Being and Time* especially Part II, sections 14-18.

15. For a treatment of culture as story or narrative structure cf. Claude Levi-Strauss, *Myth and Meaning* (New York: Schocken, 1979) and S. Crites, "The Narrative Quality of Experience," *Journal of the American Academy of Religion*, 39 (1971) 295-311.

16. Geertz, *The Interpretation of Cultures* 96.

17. *Ibid.* 97.

18. The radical variability of "human nature" over historical time and across any particular epoch is too easily overlooked; once noted it is difficult to forget. I find unforgettable presentations on this theme in John Cobb, *The Structure of Christian Existence* (Philadelphia: Westminster, 1967), a historical-comparative study of structures of human existence, and in Chapter 2 of Clifford Geertz's *The Interpretation of Cultures*, entitled "The Impact of the Concept of Culture on the Concept of Man," a searching reflection on the cultural particularity of the human.

19. Geertz, *The Interpretation of Cultures* 119.

20. In *A Rumor of Angels* (New York: Doubleday, 1969). Peter Berger analyzes the possibilities of sacred experience in contemporary society. To simplify,

his argument suggests that secular experience occurs in one finite province of meaning, sacred experience in another. In "The Narrative Quality of Experience" (see note 15 above) Crites images mundane stories as particular exemplifications of an underlying sacred story.

21. A creative theological reflection on the mystery immanent in the web of life can be found in John Shea, *Stories of God* (Chicago: Thomas More, 1978).

22. See G. and L. Lenski, *Human Societies*, 4th ed. (New York: McGraw-Hill, 1982) chap. 9.

23. On the bureaucratic form of social order see *From Max Weber: Essays in Sociology*, trans. H. Gerth and C. W. Mills (New York: Oxford, 1958) 196–244.

24. *Ibid.* 214.

25. See H. Turk, *Organizations in Modern Life* (San Francisco: Jossey-Bass, 1977).

26. See D. Macrae, *Max Weber* (New York: Viking, 1974) 95-99.

27. Weber, *Essays in Sociology* 155.

28. *Ibid.* 139.

29. This situation is thoughtfully analyzed in Morris Janowitz, *Social Control of the Welfare State* (Chicago: University of Chicago Press, 1976).

30. See R. N. Bellah et al, *Habits of the Heart* (Berkeley: University of California Press, 1985).

31. Talcott Parsons, *Personality and Social Structure* (New York: The Free Press, 1964) 196.

32. This illustration was suggested by my colleague Richard Albares.

33. In Bernard M. Loomer, "Two Conceptions of Power," *Process Studies*, 6 (1976) 5-32, the author analyzes the dynamics and effects of power conceived in traditional or unilateral terms and re-images power in relational terms.

34. The work of Jean Piaget is seminal in this regard. See, for example, *The Origins of Intelligence in Children* (New York: International University Press, 1952).

35. W. I. Thomas, *The Child in America* (New York: Knopf, 1928) 572. This statement has been described as "perhaps the only proposition in social science that approaches the status of an immutable law." In U. Bronfenbrenner, "Toward an Experimental Ecology of Human Development," *American Psychologist* (1977) 513–531.

36. On the psychoanalytic conception of transference see R. Greenson, *The Technique and Practice of Psychoanalysis* (New York: International Universities Press, 1967) 1:152-155.

37. Janet Malcom, "Profiles: The Impossible Profession," Part 1, *The New Yorker* (November 24, 1980) 56.

38. My sense of the fear of being "owned" as the dominant fear and basis for transferential responses by men in our culture has been the result of interaction with Daniel F. Carle.

39. My sense of the fear of being forgotten as the dominant fear and basis for transferential responses by women in our culture has been the result of interaction with Daniel F. Carle and Mary D. Hall.

40. The dynamics and consequences of sex-role stereotyping of our children's development is explored in Letty Cottin Pogrebin, *Growing Up Free* (New York: McGraw-Hill, 1980). I am grateful to my friend Joan Vincent for acquainting me with this work.

41. Bernard Meland, *Higher Education and the Human Spirit* (Chicago: The University of Chicago Press, 1953) chap. V.

An introduction to and commentary on Meland's "cultural theology" can be found in J. J. Mueller, *Faith and Appreciative Awareness* (Washington D.C.: University Press of America, 1981).

42. Meland, *Higher Education and the Human Spirit* 64.

43. Martin Buber, *The Knowledge of Man*, ed. M. Friedman (New York: Harper & Row, 1965) 68-69.

44. A powerful vision of Christian fidelity in an irreducibly pluralistic age can be found in John Cobb, *Christ in a Pluralistic Age* (Philadelphia: Westminster, 1975). See especially chapter 3, "Creative Transformation as the Logos."

The implications for the mutual transformation of Christianity and Buddhism are developed by John Cobb in *Beyond Dialogue* (Philadelphia: Fortress, 1982).

45. John V. Taylor, *Primal Vision* (New York: Oxford, 1963). I am grateful to my friend Barbara Strandemo for bringing this passage to my attention.

46. William Wordsworth, "Lines Above Tintern Abbey." A portion of this passage is also cited in Meland, *Higher Education and the Human Spirit* 100.

47. Patrick Kavanagh, "To a Child," *Collected Poems* (London: Martin Brian & O'Keeffe, 1964) 9.

48. Bernard Loomer has argued that ambiguity be considered a foundational metaphysical principle in *The Size of God* (William Dean, [ed.], Macon: Mercer, in press).

49. Meland, *Higher Education and the Human Spirit* 77-78.

50. Bernard Meland, *The Reawakening of Christian Faith* (New York: Macmillan, 1949) 35.

51. See, for example, T. Guzie, *Jesus and the Eucharist* (New York: Paulist Press, 1974) and Jerome Murphy-O'Connor, *Becoming Human Together* (Wilmington, Del.: Michael Glazier, 1982).

52. Meland, *The Reawakening of Christian Faith* 124-125.

Annotated References

On Meaning

Becker, Ernest. *The Birth and Death of Meaning.* 2nd ed. New York: Macmillan, 1971. Becker offers an interdisciplinary perspective on the nature of human life with meaning as the centerpiece. Drawing on anthropology, sociology, and neo-psychoanalytic psychology, he presents a vivid image of our struggles for self-esteem and significance.

Guzie, Tad. *Jesus and the Eucharist.* New York: Paulist, 1974. Guzie uses "two questions about reality"—"What is that out there?" and "What is that for man?"—to organize a detailed discussion of historical and contemporary understanding of the connection between Jesus' life and eucharistic celebration. This is a profound and highly readable text.

Langer, Suzanne, *Philosophy in a New Key.* 2nd ed. Cambridge: Mass.: Harvard, 1957. This is a most influential American philosophical work on the meaning of symbols and symbolic understanding. It holds the basic definition of symbol which was employed by Clifford Geertz in the cultural analysis of religion referred to in this essay (see "Religion as a Cultural System" below).

On Sacred Symbols

Berger, Peter. *A Rumor of Angels*. Garden City, N.Y.: Anchor, 1970 and *The Heretical Imperative*. Garden City, N.Y.: Anchor, 1980. Using the sociology-of-knowledge perspective originally presented in *The Social Construction of Reality* (with Thomas Luckmann. Garden City, N.Y.: Anchor, 1967), Berger offers a picture of the problems of socially sustaining religious experience and belief in contemporary secularized society.

Crites, Stephen. "The Narrative Quality of Experience," *Journal of the American Academy of Religion* 39 (1971) 295–311. Crites draws on a phenomenological analysis of human experience as narrative in form. He discusses the relationship between sacred (or "deep") stories and the mundane (or "surface") stories which express them. One important point made is that human beings do not, indeed cannot, deliberately or instrumentally fashion sacred stories.

Meland, Bernard. *The Realities of Faith*. New York: Oxford, 1962; *Faith and Culture*. Carbondale, Ill.: Southern Illinois University Press, 1953; and *Fallible Forms and Symbols*. Philadelphia: Fortress, 1976. In this trilogy Meland develops an analysis of the interpenetration of theology and culture with considerable significance for religious (including liturgical) experience in our time. The texts reflect significant appreciation of contemporary cultural anthropology and of religious experience in other cultures.

Shea, John. *Stories of God*. Chicago: Thomas More, 1978. Shea takes up the narrative perspective for theological reflection on Christian stories of hope and justice, trust and freedom, and invitation and decision. In an especially fine chapter entitled "World-making," Shea captures the centrality of meaning for human life with elegance and depth.

On Culture

Bellah, Robert N. et al. *Habits of the Heart*. Berkeley: University of California Press, 1985. In this informative and easily accessible work Bellah and his associates analyze both classic texts of American culture and interviews with individuals. Their reflection on patterns of individualism and commitment in American life bids fair to become a classic in its own right. Readers of this series may be particularly interested in the authors' assessment in chapter 9 of the ambiguous effects of religion on individualism in the American cultural experience.

Geertz, Clifford. *The Interpretation of Cultures*. New York: Basic Books, 1973. The Geertz essay from this collection entitled "Religion as a Cultural System" is the central anthropological resource for the preceding essay. It also contains the anthropological definition of religion perhaps most frequently cited by contemporary theologians (page 90). Another essay on religion in the collection, "Ethos, World View, and the Analysis of Sacred Symbols," develops Geertz's semiotic analysis of religious symbols. The essay which introduces the collection, "Thick Description: Toward an Interpretative Theory of Culture," is a classic statement of the tenets of a semiotic or meaning-based theory of the workings of culture.

Levi-Strauss, Claude. *Myth and Meaning*. New York: Schocken, 1979. This is an extremely readable basic statement of the structuralist anthropological analysis of culture. The origin of meanings in mythical stories of origin is central in this perspective on culture. Levi-Strauss deals in the text with myth and science, myth and history, and myth and music.

On Society

Lenski, Gerhard and Jean. *Human Societies.* 4th ed. New York: McGraw-Hill, 1982. This introductory sociology text gives a comprehensive introduction to the anatomy and evolution of macrosocial structure. It is a very useful entry point to the world of social analysis, especially for persons whose ways of understanding human life have been primarily oriented to individuals and their feelings, beliefs, and behaviors. After examining the theoretical foundations of sociological analysis, the authors apply those perspectives first to preindustrial and then to industrial and industrializing societies.

Mills, C. Wright. *The Sociological Imagination* (New York: Oxford, 1959). This work by a trenchant critic of American society takes the reader into social reflection on the concrete events of our world. Mills stresses the importance of distinguishing between individual problems and issues in living which reflect the character of social reality in particular societies. The former calls for a psychological, and the latter for a sociological, imagination.

Turk, Herman. *Organizations in Modern Life.* San Francisco: Jossey-Bass, 1977. In this work Turk looks on society as an aggregate of large-scale organizations. He analyzes the patterns of interdependence among large social networks and shows the processes that link up the massive bureaucratic substructures of advanced industrial society.

Weber, Max. From *Max Weber: Essays in Sociology*, trans. Hans Gerth and C. Wright Mills. New York: Oxford, 1958. In these essays Weber, the great analyst and prophetic critic of Western civilization, offers reflections on science and politics, power, religion, and social structures. Of particular interest to readers of the preceding essay may be his reflections on bureaucracy in Part II, Chapter VIII.

2. READINESS FOR RITUAL:
PSYCHOLOGICAL ASPECTS OF MATURITY IN CHRISTIAN CELEBRATION

Paul J. Philibert, O.P.

Introduction

CONNECTING EVERYDAY REALITY WITH RITUAL LIFE

This book sets out different perspectives upon sacraments in the Christian life. Questions of history, theology, psychology, sociology, and anthropology are addressed here. But underlying all the particular perspectives there is a common problem of *meaning.*[1]

As adults all of us have occasional moments when we wonder what is going on in our lives. Sometimes we have trouble finding meaning *within* the repeated chores of day-to-day reality; at other times it is meaning *beyond* the day-to-day that is hard to find. We get restless when things feel confused or unfocused. Perhaps we promise ourselves a vacation or a holiday a couple of months ahead, and that promise becomes *a symbol* of liberation, expressing our hope that we can endure, at least until the moment of freedom. Perhaps we choose to search for the sense of what we are doing in intimate conversation with someone who loves us, and that sharing of burdens becomes a symbol that we are not alone. Liberation and communion, expressed in everyday reality through dreams and conversations, are empowering symbols.

Christian symbols, on the other hand, do not always convey the immediacy or vitality of liberation and communion. Their vitality will depend upon the connection we are able to make between everyday life and our community's ritual life. For instance, adults can treat Sunday worship like a sacred parenthesis that has nothing to do with the rest of their lives; in such a case there is no need for a connection. Then Christian symbols would be arbitrary consumer goods, taken at face value as odd moments of word and gesture commanded by divine law. On the contrary, Christian symbols can be instead a magnifying lens through which the meanings of ordinary life become enlarged to the point of bringing into focus the gnawing uncertainties that often trouble any thoughtful believer. This book is devoted to the task of presenting ideas that flow out of the dynamic, inclusive point of view that Christian symbols magnify life's day-to-day meanings.

A number of truths emerge from taking this point of view. Here are some: the Christian celebration of sacraments is not utterly unlike other moments in human life; sacraments, too, are a building up of meaning in the active, searching lives of people whose frontiers of meaning are always moving further ahead of them. Liturgical gestures are not the only ritual dimensions of our lives; our lives are filled with rituals. Most of them go unnoticed because they are habitual and so strategic in providing meaning to our passing days. Moreover, the true "subject" of liturgical experience is not an individual, but a community; communities co-construct meanings in repeated efforts to explain the point of what we do and what we are.[2]

While these perspectives fit fairly well into all of the writing that follows, they take on different moods or feelings, depending on the way they are highlighted. What follows immediately is a brief discussion of differences between an individual-psychological focus and a communal-sociological focus. This discussion is introduced by way of some observations which remark upon the diverse interests of theology and the social sciences.

The Interests of the Social Sciences and of Theology

The relation between theology and the social sciences is an important background for the issues which we will discuss. This book is about sacraments as actions in a community, as ritual behavior, and as revealing signs. At one level I wish to point out the diversity of meanings which reside in familiar religious activity. There is more here than meets the eye, one might say.

At another level I wish to highlight some of these meanings as being especially important. Here is where the social sciences come in. For instance psychology can tell us about typical patterns of ideas which occur in all of us in response to our relationships and our environment. These patterns have a range of expression, running from positive and empowering ideas to negative and draining ideas. Such patterns, which express our overall attitude toward reality, have an influence upon our ideas about God, as well as about other things within our day-to-day experience. In fact one of the most important contributions which psychology offers to theology is a persuasive argument that all our ideas are dynamic instead of static; they are constantly shifting and exploring for meaning, instead of fixed and closed.

On the other hand, sociology and anthropology look for patterns within the typical arrangements of institutions and human associations. Some meanings, generally hidden beneath the familiarity of customary behavior, provide new depth of understanding when brought to light and examined in terms of our everchanging human situations. People characteristically fail to realize that a great deal of what feels personally important to them in fact arises out of attitudes, interests, and values shared within networks of civic, religious, or family relationships. Such relationships offer an identity; they tell us implicitly, "I belong." Such "belonging" not only provides a comforting sense of being in the right place, but also supplies a set of characteristic ways of looking at things. Our general expectations of life emerge out of such a network of sharing.

By social sciences my reference is principally to psychology, sociology, and anthropology where developmental issues are central to human understanding. Politics, economics, and history are also included. What all these branches of study have in common is an interest in society as a context for human interaction. Most of the social sciences were developed within the last 150 years, so from a historical perspective they are all very recent. Consequently, it is not surprising that, on the one hand, some of their findings are considered quite tentative while, on the other hand, their mutually supporting perspectives have not been brought into an adequate synthesis yet. I think that there is great scope for enriching our understanding of Christian sacraments by pulling together ideas and insights which come from a variety of social science perspectives.[3]

A conversation which exchanges points of view between theology and the social sciences requires special attention. The rules for inquiry and conversation vary considerably between theology and the sciences. While at a popular level certain ideas appear to interact freely and constructively—for example, both sides talk about ideas named freedom, goals, human good, or community—their breadth of meaning is bound to vary from one side to the other.

This variation in meaning is the result of different rules or methodology for inquiry and conversation. The social sciences for their part aim to limit themselves to an objective examination of facts. In science facts are the product of an inquiry which conforms to the methodology of rigorous observation: facts are observable, measurable, and repeatable. Scientific facts, then, tend to be a sort of generalized summary of what appears to be universally true for particular classes of things. Social science methodology for its part strives to be very open and articulate about its assumptions. A particular investigation rests upon previously established facts or upon certain hypotheses whose probability will be tested in research. In any case, like the hard sciences the social sciences aim to be reasonable. They aim to achieve a rational clarity which any fair-minded individual should be able to follow.

There are some differences, however, between societal and individual perspectives within the social sciences. A typical sociological perspective would want to emphasize the back and forth movement between personal initiative and societal context. Peter Berger's formula is: "Man is the product of society; but society is also a human product."[4] While valuable insights may be derived from such a starting point, this focus nonetheless tends to neglect the expanding frame of reference of the individual subject. A developmental psychologist is far more concerned about the influence of stages of development on a person's readiness to understand and act than about the complexity of the stimuli which form the individual's situation (although, of course, neither psychologists nor sociologists blithely dismiss either development or situation).

This leads me to observe that another foundational difference in perspective might be described this way. The sociologist is likely to take socialized adults interacting within a group system as the subject of inquiry. On the other hand, the psychologist will more likely maintain a developmental perspective which starts with infancy, remembering that individual subjects differ in consequence of their developing understandings and changing experiences.[5]

THEOLOGY'S APPROACH

The methodology of theology, while similar in many respects to the sciences, differs significantly. Theology is distinctive for its starting point, which is faith. Faith is a believer's response to God's self-revelation. The Christian community maintains its memory of God's revelation through the reading and proclamation of the Bible. The Bible calls forth faith from a believer when God's biblical word is accompanied by a movement of the Holy Spirit, often consciously perceived as a moment of religious experience. Thus the Bible and religious experience are the two principal sources for the awakening of faith, which stands at the beginning of theology.[6]

The Bible, received by the Church as the revealed word of God, provides keys to human meaning which reach into the inaccessible darkness of a prehistoric past and into the equally inaccessible light of an eternal future. Although the Bible's language is a special, symbolic language, developed inside a community of people who know they have a special intimacy and destiny with God, it still tells us trustworthy secrets about our origin, our human dignity, and our destiny. These are things which lie beyond the reach of the sciences, whose frontiers are bounded by the observable. Sometimes individual practitioners of the social sciences observe in themselves or in others phenomena which seem to overlap with the religious questions of the Bible. When that happens, and it seems to be happening more frequently all the time, conversation between theologians and scientists becomes particularly interesting.

Theology also considers religious experience seriously. Religious experience here means a moment of knowing and feeling which carries someone beyond the ordinary limits of their everyday world of meaning. Religious experience either calls someone to faith or confirms them in an existing faith. It provides an undeniable confrontation with the horizon within which familiar concerns of life go on. It is a kind of awakening to the uncontrollable scope of reality.

Powerful experiences of beauty or power or surprise can shake up someone to the point of requiring a profound and lasting readjustment in what they imagine to be the shape and dimensions of reality. A lot of people have been called to faith at the edge of the Grand Canyon or, as St. Augustine was, walking on the seashore. The impact of awesome beauty triggers a realization that one's ideas of what's real are altogether too narrow. Such a moment, whether an event of nature or a loving relationship, becomes effectively a call to faith. Similar experiences throughout life confirm and consolidate faith's understanding. St. Paul talks about being anointed by the Holy Spirit, which seems to be a metaphor for the experience of having one's faith confirmed in some moment of wonder and adoration.

Such experiences are looked at in very different ways in the sciences and in theology. The sciences choose to focus upon observable causes of a person's special feeling in such moments. Theology is more inclined to focus upon the way such moments bring to experience the divine promises contained in the Bible. Indeed, even though the theologian constantly looks beyond the Bible for understanding, the Bible remains the core of the theologian's interest. God's word is like the center of gravity of the space wherein theology takes place.

It should be noted that religious experience of another sort flows throughout life as a continuing process by which an individual is gradually incorporated into the faith outlook of a believing community. This other day-to-day awareness of the divine as the loving source of ordinary reality provides the most common and frequent dimension of the presence of God that most of us know as we celebrate liturgy.

SIGN AND SACRAMENT

The central terminology used here is a matter of special concern. Words which are popularly used in very similar ways can have different connotations. The distinction between sign and symbol is an example.

One difference between sign and symbol is a difference in perspective. A sign is matter-of-fact, anybody's sign; a symbol is deeply personal: much of its meaning comes from my own reservoir of needs and feelings. This is why sign is the most general of the words used to speak of things which take the place in meaning of something else signified. A stop sign is very objective; impersonal, direct, simple, it signifies *warning*—someone knows a dangerous situation exists—and *command*—someone has the authority to insist upon the directive to stop.

The word sign might also be used of other incidents such as Judas' kiss of betrayal or even for the breaking of the bread. But then sign is too general a word, because it leaves out of consideration the personal elements which constitute the special precinct of the symbolic.

Symbols, which like signs include the factor of "re-presentation" of some other reality, go deeper than signs. This is because symbols draw upon elusive meaning which is at home in memory and imagination and which cannot be made matter-of-factly articulate, said, and then passed over. We linger in memory and imagination upon symbols of sharing, of love, and of achievement like letters from loved ones or trophies and prizes. It would be quite odd to linger in the same way over a sign like a soup can label or a stop sign on a roadway.[7]

Signs give us all there is to be said or done in a given situation. In symbols we contribute at least half the meaning and action. Ritual broadly means in our context the pulling together of symbolic actions into the form of a story or explanation about our life's meanings. In family life we do this every time we get out the photo album or home movies. Elder persons in families can be counted on to retell the same stories over and over. Remembering the family's stories is a kind of ritual re-membering of the participants into a single social unit.

Religious symbols are meant to have this same kind of immediacy. Clearly they often do not.

PROBLEMS WITH RELIGIOUS RITUALS AND SYMBOLS

When we look at other aspects of adult life, we can easily note that adults typically interact with ideas and prospects in a creative, cooperative way. The world of commerce makes every effort to sell the notion that a product is "customized" to meet the personal desires of a discerning or demanding individual. Adults in conversation exchange a give-and-take in a process which leads to shared understanding and consent. In the light of this characteristically "active" posture of adults before most of their significant choices, it is noteworthy when we find adults in "passive" attitudes before religious activity and worship.

One of the chief things which I hope to explain is the irony that adults seem so often to become passive nonparticipants in religious rituals at the very point that their participation should be decisive. They become consumers of a symbolic reality which is incomplete without the testimony of their own memory and imagination. Too often Sunday worship in the parish becomes a "franchise" in some sort of supernatural consumerism.

A consumer attitude, however, is just what developmental studies are eager to explode. Erikson's treatment of adolescent, young adult, and adult developmental tasks gives an example of this.[8] Adolescence, in Erikson's view, provokes the personal construction of a distinctive sense of oneself and one's destiny as a unique person. Certainly, the range of options which anyone will explore will be influenced by their raw materials and by available reality. But what the developmental task is all about is getting beneath socially given roles and the available raw materials. Much the same is true at the next level of the life cycle, when it comes to intimacy.

Erikson treats intimacy as a challenge to individuals to get beyond the limitations of superficial roles or of conventional expectations to a sense of respect for the unique selves that the persons are as creative beings. While the persons in question are shaped by the "raw materials" of social role and expectations for making meaning, the developmental task of intimacy is to transcend those precise limitations. By transcend in this case, I mean that two individuals cooperating toward intimate mutual understanding achieve their goal at the point where they realize that each of them is more than the roles they play socially and more than the roles which they have used to interpret their presence to one another.

The midadult developmental task of generativity also has something of this aspect of going beyond mere social conformity. Once adults have dealt with their responsibilities to continue the family line, produce offspring, and nurture them into some kind of autonomy, they need to reorientate their responsibilities. They do this by reaching beyond the boundaries of family and strict role expectations in order to construct a sense of responsibility for the future of their society. Ancient Rome used to call this *pietas:* a mixture of respect and gratitude for their own roots leading adults to a concern for the successful future of their community and culture.

Each of these postadolescent dimensions of Erikson's life cycle suggests something common in the inclinations toward identity, intimacy, and generativity. In all three cases Erikson is attempting to describe something "given" in the orientation of the adult human personality. There is a fundamental human hunger for integrity of meaning. Despite the materialistic influences of our culture, we are able to draw upon the undeniable *eros* (radical hunger) of the human personality for authentic meaning. One person's integrity is perhaps another person's cop-out. Developmental tasks always involve negotiations which build upon the inherent limitations and capacities of people in unique situations. Nonetheless each person knows some dimension of restless yearning *(eros)* which urges one on beyond conformity.[9]

Our society has been labelled a consumer society for over twenty-five years. The thrust of that label is to suggest that Americans have become dependent upon merchandizing and advertising to control their interests and desires. Media appeals have the power to generate artificial needs and likewise to deemphasize or eliminate the feeling for natural goods. Fast food chains serve as an example: the gathering of family around a table laid with lovingly prepared dishes is replaced by a quick in-and-out experience where speed supersedes nutrition and community. Some human values depend upon a gradual build up of feeling for them; loving relations take time and caring. So it seems that a major drift in American society is away from human values and symbolic appreciation in ordinary day-to-day living.

On the other hand, good ritual celebration—good symbols, we might say—ought to be able to arouse a desire for personal meaning and to call upon symbolic hungers in memory and imagination. However, some authors tell us that in the post Second Vatican Council renewal period, liturgical celebrations have become more prosaic than ever. Everything is explained in a flat, wordy prose uniform in its dullness.[10] If this is true to any great extent, then it is not surprising that the symbolic dimensions of celebration do not emerge in a compelling fashion for many Catholics. Instead of experiencing Sunday Mass as an opportunity for reinterpreting the meaning of their lives in the light of the shared story of Jesus of Nazareth, they more likely experience Mass as an impenetrable ritual action demanded as a price for belonging to the Church.

Going Deeper into Meaning

Nowadays the term "deep stories" is used to suggest the dimension at which we interpret our story by the story of Jesus. This term implies that communication occurs at levels well beneath the surface of day-to-day conversation and analysis. Some symbolic dynamic in celebration touches some hidden need or hunger in the worshipper.[11] Even here there is a difference of perspective between the approach of sociology and of psychology.

Sociology looks for preunderstandings characteristic of a given society. Preunderstanding means vague or unspoken tendencies which influence the way we bring something to meaning. For example a society's tendency to seek out retribution for unfairness functions as a preunderstanding. Regardless of the content of a story in the concrete, this inclination toward reestablishing fairness will control the feelings, concepts, language, and actions which express the human narrative. Liturgy *fails* when the gospel stories are simply perceived as repeated familiar tales, heard year after year, with the flatness of yesterday's newspaper. Liturgy *succeeds* only when the gospel stories are recognized as treasuries of life-giving preunderstandings which connect us in imagination and in desire with the promises of God's kingdom preached by Jesus.

Psychology, on the other hand, takes a different point of departure. Following Freud, psychology investigates the personal unconscious through the techniques of free association, dream study, and the retrieval of traumatic events from the past. The direction of our lives may be owed as fully to the tacit intentions of our unconscious as to the reasonable decisions of our conscious discernments. If this is so, then a sociological repertory of deep stories (which Jung would have called the "collective unconscious") is interesting but not decisive. What is more likely to be decisive is the drive for meaning that stems from the themes of incompleteness, woundedness, or destiny which pulse beneath the rational surface of our conscious experience.

So a societal perspective in the first instance goes along the byways of myth, primordial story, and symbol systems. Sociology and anthropology are concerned to name the reality which serves as the destination of our journey into fullness of meaning. In the second instance psychology goes along the path of *eros*. Eros is a way of speaking about the unlimited hunger of humans for meaning, a search for completeness and wholeness. We are hungry for unconditional acceptance, intimate mutuality, healing of unconscious wounds, and all the beauty that there is. Different theorists will name these dimensions of eros in different ways, but they will all be speaking about the hunger for meaning as a radical component of human awareness.[12]

Once again liturgy *fails* when it becomes merely a duty in the present, instead of a symbolic foretaste of the satisfaction of our human hungers. For this foretaste to occur, we need to be wise about the relative worth of the many shallow pleasures that swallow up our moral energies. We also need to find celebrations which render the Jesus story and its promise for us plausible and credible in a world of no-nonsense practicality.

What Is Wrong in Celebration?

There are, then, two answers to the question: what's wrong in Catholic sacramental celebration? One says our culture is teaching us to be insensitive to the subtle dimensions of human symbols, so that the sharing of hungers and of satisfying joys is lost in the pursuit of efficiency, ease, and mindless excitation. Another answer says our celebrations are themselves flat, unimaginative, and impersonal; they seldom evoke a fullness of meaning beyond the trotting out of words and repeated gestures. They pall in their overfamiliarity.

Psychology proposes some important insights here. The rituals and symbols of a community are internalized in a complex process. The individual is caught up in a twofold process of community self-expression and of wider cultural belonging. Young children imitate the symbolic actions which identify people as belonging to "this kind" of community well before they understand the rites or the ritual words. Children are eager to be with and to be identified with attractive adults. All of us, therefore, begin our experience of religious and sacramental life as hangers-on: participants at the periphery who consume the awesome words and gestures of adults as something just like magic.[13]

Faith development studies tell us that there is an awkward in-between period, when youth are critical of the naive dependency of their earliest religious life. This critical moment is awkward because at this point youth do not yet feel a need for adult symbols. J. W. Fowler calls this his stage four of faith development. It is a time when someone wants everything to be clear, rational, functional, and exact. This stage can last for a very long time in a person's attitudes. It requires a certain number of "failures" to lead a person into the ambiguity that demands a new season of symbols. These could be called *personal symbols* or symbols which "put things back together again." In this sense the word symbol has both a naive and an adult meaning.[14]

Adult or personal symbols can be places, persons, events, remembered moments—a vast range of things and experiences. I think of them as notable markers of the way the fullness of life has been unforgettably revealed to us as individuals. For example, lovers have special places where they remember first saying "I love you:" such a place is a personal symbol. A book or an author whose writing discloses answers to enduring questions can become a personal symbol, as Teilhard de Chardin became for many Catholics in the 1960's and 1970's. A prophetic figure like Mother Teresa can be a personal symbol, signifying that society's abandonment of the poor, one of the most painful realities of our era, need not be a dead end.

In adulthood the celebrating community's rituals need to invite an awareness and a celebration of personal symbols. This does not need to be done through the individual public witness of each member's special insights or wondrous moments; most people seem to feel that their personal symbols are too precious and intimate to be paraded in public. Rather it is done through the development in celebration and preaching of a wide-ranging symbolic awareness: language which respects diversity of interests and gifts, rites which make connections with day-to-day events, and nonverbal sharings of gestures and silences which allow the divine rites to flow imaginatively into the reflective awareness of the worshippers. The notion of symbolic competence which is used later on has as a central meaning the capacity to connect traditional and biblical symbols with the adult, personal symbols of the worshippers.

Another important insight which psychology may offer deals with the static that may result when two sets of cultural expectations, dissonant in their values, try to merge. What I have in mind is the conflict between a gospel ethic and a Playboy ethic. Most television situation comedies seem to reflect the Playboy ethic that life is about the lighthearted pursuit of pleasure. Most Catholic preaching seems to moralize about desirable themes of generosity without confronting head-on the dissonance. The result is likely to produce a ho-hum reaction: the preacher is out of touch, unrealistic, or does not know what is going on.

Tuning out or turning off is the easy way out, when the demands of the Christian message are not made clear. But developmental psychology, following Piaget and Kohlberg, acknowledges that focused discomfort with available reality—what psychology calls "cognitive dissonance"—is the major stimulus to growth in psychological understanding. So, for instance, a community which coexists with the unquestioned ambiguity promoted by the arms race economy—deferring responsibility across the board to federal authorities—is less likely to stimulate growth or community-identification than another community which tries to articulate Christian values about such an issue. The American Bishops' Pastoral Letter on this issue has been criticized for being divisive. The Bishops' letter discriminates between those who simply take their values from the prevailing drift of the secular culture and those who at some point acknowledge the binding force of gospel values. Unless we go to pains to make the point explicitly, it will be lost upon Catholics that Christian attitudes are quite often the polar opposite of the Playboy ethic. Saying nothing about the big issues encourages muddling around in a world where few values are articulate. That is disastrous.[15]

In such a situation I see the central task of adult Christian living as the increasingly articulate expression of values which are drawn from the Jesus story and from the Christian community. Adult living becomes increasingly symbolic not by withdrawing from the secular world into a world of religious icons, but by manifesting personal faith in Christian integrity. Far from fearing that an articulate challenge of the media's materialism and hedonism will drive Christians from their churches, we would do better to express vividly concrete images of what we imagine Christian fellowship and service to look like in the world we share.

THEOLOGICAL IMAGERY FROM THE POPULAR CULTURE

My guess is that theologians have a lot to learn from popular culture. We need to learn about where people's questions lie. We need to learn how to sustain imagery by expanding rather than constricting the scope of its meaning. The secular symbols of *Star Wars*, ritualizing the "Force" as an oblique theological reference to the origin and destiny of reality, demonstrate the resilience of *ultimate* human questions. The "Force" is a new kind of God-talk, which aims to go beyond the parochial limits of childhood socialization to express transcendence in the scope of intergalactic society and to affirm hope that ultimate meaning still lies beyond the frontiers of technological manipulation of the physical world.

It is the work of poets and artists to inhabit the middle world between tacit hungers and articulate categories. But that is what the world of symbolism is all about. At the tacit dimension meaning feels like a hunger in the gut—for love, for significance, for meaning. We too easily domesticate the questing and yearning for the deep experiences of faith by naming the components with static categories. Often poets have been better at celebrating the shadow world between hunger and healing than have an older cast of theologians.[16]

Part of the task of liturgical renewal is redefining the religious expectations that the Church has of adult believers. The healthy faith of a Christian adult is not the static security of someone who has "settled down" but the "responsible restlessness" of someone who realizes that our hearts will not rest until they rest in the nameless divine love who has been revealed to us by Jesus under the privileged image of "Father."

Before I pass on to a description of a typical journey of growth in the Christian life, it should be clear that good liturgy is not a matter alone of the *right things* or even of the *right happenings*, though both are clearly important. It is also a matter of personal readiness to *see, respond, interpret*, and *cooperate* in actions which build a fundamentally new perspective on life, a "new creation."

Christian Celebration and the Question of Readiness

Each person has authentic needs which are met by the proclamation of God's eternal love, by the mystery of the communion of saints, and by the sharing of holy signs that convince us of our safe passage into eternal life. Consequently the Church's proclamation about these "divine" dimensions of human living can be powerfully effective.

Yet there are obstacles which impede the effectiveness of the Church's proclamation. Such obstacles are a part of everyone's experience. At some point in each life, any man or woman must deal with feelings about themselves as unworthy or unloved in particular situations. All children at some point experience the surprise and pain of finding that no one—or, at least, not the right ones—know them and accept them quite the way they think they need to be known and accepted. Even in an overwhelmingly positive environment of loving family and caring friends, such moments of disappointment make their impact on the personality. Out of such moments come characteristic ideas of God which are inappropriate, narrow, or incorrect, even though generated in response to early childhood experience. Such inappropriate ideas of God, when long-established and familiar, are often difficult to uproot or replace.

Another obstacle is the adult's failure to utilize the full scope of memory and imagination in theological thinking and ritual expression. There is significant adult learning in the realms of symbol and celebration. Unfortunately, many adults imagine that their preparation for Christian celebration has reached its completion by the time they graduate into high school. The present examination of symbolic competence ought to disqualify such an idea.

Therefore, it is not implausible to speak of readiness for Christian celebration or of symbolic competence. In the following pages I am concerned with the range of human presence which Christians bring to the Church's proclamation of divine mysteries and with their response to that proclamation. Typical patterns of growth from childhood into adulthood will help us to see the foundations for adult symbolic competence.

SYMBOLS AND CHRISTIAN CELEBRATION

The focus here of my concern with symbol is the individual person's readiness to perceive the full scope of a symbolic action, rite, or object. Ritual symbols offer historical continuity with the Christian tradition. They also render us aware of the presence of God, who remains among us and calls us into communion.

Such ritual symbols entail a bewildering plurality of interwoven dimensions, all of which bear on the range of symbolic meaning. Symbols possess many qualities; they are archaic, complex, and many-dimensioned. Each of these aspects of ritual symbols creates an ambiguity in that it is possible for someone to affirm a part of symbolic meaning and still deny other aspects of the symbol. Briefly, these multiple qualities are the following.

Ritual symbols are archaic. In Christian celebration symbols are used for the purpose of evoking a present participation in a promise which God made long ago. We meet God through symbols, using gestures established centuries ago by our fathers and mothers in faith. We break bread and share the cup today, remembering Jesus, because the first generation of believers who followed the preaching of Jesus remembered him and what he did and taught. Yet, in the first Christian century they themselves drew upon ancient practices of the Jewish religion, using already archaic rites for the sharing of communion meals which remembered God's deliverance of his chosen people. Even in our reading of the Gospel, the Christian Church has characteristically used the formula, *"In illo tempore,"* that is, "At that time." Symbols have the power to transport us out of the here and now into an originating past as well as into a fulfilling future.

When we fail to respect the archaic character of the rite, we collapse the tension between the present historic moment of celebration and the past originating moment of divine institution. This can lead to a terrible flattening of ritual experience. The resurrection of Jesus, which is the source of all the sacraments' transforming power, is the key event which transcends time. Precisely because it has both a dimension of "then" (while Jesus passed from actual dying to new life) and a dimension of "now" (when Jesus breaks in upon our today through faith), the resurrection empowers ritual remembrance with a true participation in Christ's new life. Further, it is meaningful and empowering to situate ourselves alongside the centuries of believers who join us in understanding through the power of ritual symbols, despite the chasm of centuries and the disparity of cultural environment. Although symbols are archaic, we use them in the historical present. Therefore the tension between *then* and *now* is inescapable, if ritual symbol is to exploit its full potential.[17]

Symbols are complex. Generally in Christian celebration, ritual symbols are expressed within an environment created by a composite grouping of symbolic acts and objects. We create a particular space for celebration by bringing together many elements which mutually enhance one another. Among those we can think of are locations set apart by icons, banners, altars, or ceremonial space; spatial focus created by lighting, especially the use of candles and lamps; and the production of a sense of community through the binding power of song and spoken response in a gathered assembly. Dozens of other forms of ritual and symbolic expression combine to produce a unified experience. Special gestures, ornamented plates, bowls, and cups, and the use of characteristic musical instruments and melodies all have the capacity to evoke the presence of God. An eye too familiar with these things can become blind, an ear too accustomed, deaf to the meaning which reposes in this great complexity of symbolic forms.[18]

This complex process of evoking a "space for God" by building a texture of visual and acoustical specialness ironically can either distance us from a sense of God's presence or awaken a sense of divine immediacy. Here is a case where we "see through" the symbols in a double sense: in one sense we "see by way of" symbols as objects which stimulate religious experience; in another sense we "see beyond" symbols which, in their material reality, yield to divine fullness beyond visible expression. The complex of symbols evokes, rather, an attitude of faith which is able to surrender to the God present but hidden, revealing himself at a depth we cannot easily describe.

Symbols are many-dimensioned. It is easy for the child to perceive, first of all, that ritual symbols are "things which our people do." That is, just as any family takes for granted the range of cuisine characteristic of its ethnic heritage, so any community takes for granted the symbolic expression characteristic of its religious tradition.

In addition there is the question of a symbol's natural depths. Ritual symbols characteristically respond to deep imaginative needs and intentions which are not easily transformed directly into common language. Water as a symbol expresses not only the functional meaning of washing or wetting, slaking thirst, or refreshing the hot and tired traveler. Water also says something to the "depths" of any person, psychically situating the participant within a world vast enough to include the only vaguely remembered infinite origins of one's eternal beginnings.

Carl Jung is the twentieth-century spokesman for this mysterious dimension of symbols. Within his theory of "archetypes" is included the assertion that many "natural symbols" such as water, fire, a breeze, or a cup of wine, contain meanings which can never be fully articulated in common language. These many meanings are mysteriously evoked and affirmed in the presentation and sharing of objects and actions which give rise to a special open, accepting quality of consciousness and attention. It is, then, important to become aware that bread is a natural symbol well before it is taken in hand in preparation for the Christian Eucharist. It is likewise important that water be known as an element which has something to say to our depths about the origin of life and the threat of death before we begin intending to initiate someone into the Christian mystery of eternal life.[19]

In this perspective one aspect of "symbolic competence" will be to overcome the flattening out of symbols whereby only immediate, concrete, and matter-of-fact aspects of objects, words, and rites come to light. Competence here includes readiness to succumb to the subtle feelings, attitudes, or expectations which are properly awakened when natural symbols speak directly to the subconscious layers of mind.

Symbolic and Diabolic Orientations of Ritual Signs

So symbols are realities which are only partly articulate. At their best they point immediately away from themselves toward a deeper reality which can only be perceived in the shared depths of the Holy Spirit. Therefore to treat symbols as absolute in the present is to go against the nature of things. Ritual symbolic action, even when drawing upon a sacred tradition, is always somehow spontaneous and free. Ritual life is also part of a present historic moment, which means that customary expressions can become outdated and empty. To take symbolic expression out of the framework of contemporary existence reduces our living venture into the world between mystery and speech into a simple rote performance of a sacred script.

It was certainly with dynamics such as these in mind that the Bishops' Committee on the Liturgy in 1972 published the following statement: "Good celebrations foster and nourish faith. Poor celebrations weaken and destroy faith."[20] The committee was clearly aware that they were speaking of Christian ritual celebration, but they refused to consider exclusively the matter-of-fact objective dimension of that celebration. They insisted upon the need for interiority, the challenge of living faith, and the building of a community of justice and fellowship. To develop a shorthand for the statement of the Bishops' Committee, I will be speaking in these pages of the *symbolic* and *diabolic* orientations of ritual signs. These are my terms to designate the constructive and the constrictive use of sacramental symbolism.

Edward Kilmartin will explain later in this volume how he sees the believers themselves, participating in the Church's worship, as the sacrament from which a community's sacramental actions derive. His theological account reflects the dynamic of what I mean here by a *symbolic* orientation. The eternally holy appears within the present, ordinary human situation. The gestures we use today are constructive of an event in which ancient promises and eternal communion become contemporary to us. Because such notions are foundational for a theology of sacraments, I consider it important to dwell on the contrary dynamics of the *symbolic* and the *diabolic* in religious ritual action.

Symbolic and Diabolic

An overdrawn example of what I mean by a diabolic orientation in ritual life is a purely obedience/punishment motivation for going to Sunday Mass. The gathering of God's people becomes a reluctant captive audience; the bringing and sharing of the gifts of life become an unwelcome interruption in the course of everyday life. The symbol becomes gutted of meaning and is replaced with negative dynamics and threats. The Banquet of the Lord becomes a penance. It will become clear that I am using the word diabolic in a special sense; one, however, which is authentic in terms of the development of language.

The word symbol seems to have been used in ancient times for an object much like today's passport. When a messenger bearing important information was sent to an authority or official, he was given a piece of a broken tablet which would identify himself as authorized when that piece was placed together with another matching piece in the possession of the official. Originally a Greek word, symbol (*sum-ballein*) meant to pull together aspects which have either been broken apart, sundered, or which have yet to find a synthetic fullness in being united. Diabolic is another word which comes from the Greek language. It is similar in construction, although opposite in meaning. Diabolic means the breaking apart of something. We are accustomed to using this word exclusively in terms of its association with the devil. But in ancient usage, the devil was a translation of the Hebrew *satan*, a word meaning adversary, one who breaks apart our peace and unity. I intend to exploit the diametrically opposed meanings of the symbolic and the diabolic. In doing so, I hope to find a way to express the fragility of cosmic, transcendent symbolic experience.[21]

Symbols as symbolic pull together the vision of the community and its traditions and history with the ordinary experiences of everyday. They allow us to *be* in a world of simple desire, interpretive ambiguity, indigenous cultural expression, and random significance and still connect our experiences and desires with the holy communion of God's chosen, but ordinary people. Symbols as symbolic connect up the reality of God as our present source of life with the reality of our day-to-day experience. When Eucharist as a symbol functions *symbolically*, the Bread of Life and the Cup of Salvation become our daily bread; valuing, endorsing, and assuaging the specific hungers of our own moment of time and our own particular present needs.

By contrast, symbols function diabolically when they sunder apart the tradition of the community from the ordinary experience of everyday. When ritual actions become absolute and perfectionistic, impatient of ambiguity, and divisive, then the present needs of real people are irrelevant and unimportant. Symbols as diabolic cast the Originating Real apart from the experienced real. This leaves our reality unredeemed and indifferent, and ourselves thereby isolated and impersonal.

Ritual symbols function diabolically also when they are co-opted by sexism, colonialism, cultural domination, social injustice, and racial alienation. Clericalism understood as the unwarranted use of authority to dominate others in nonhierarchical roles is another example of diabolical symbolism. In any cases where Christian celebration is at issue, the proclamation of the gospel of peace and the sharing of the Bread of Life are used diabolically not to break down barriers, but to reinforce them; not to build structures of communion, but bonds of constraint.[22] Diabolic celebration of ritual symbols produces an *incarceration* of the participants within a timeless parenthesis of formalized and abstracted actions, rather than an *incarnation* of the participants' shared hopes and values in a revealing moment of insight and possibility.

The source for diabolic uses of Christian ritual symbols can be found in a review of the developmental factors in psychological growth. At the far end of this review, I will claim that an adult readiness for Christian ritual will be symbolic in the sense that it pulls divine promises together with human experience in such a way as to be liberating and creative. This review will allow us to see that no part of adult living, secular or religious, can reach mature scope without all of the building blocks of symbolic competence.

Ritualization as the Framework of Personal Growth

THE MEANINGS OF RITUALIZATION

In his book *Toys and Reasons* psychologist Erik Erikson developed the argument that newborn human children become acquainted with the way of doing things common in their culture through the framework of ritualization. Erikson's phrase for this is the "ontogeny of ritualization"—a phrase which needs some explanation. The word ontogeny comes from two Greek words *ontos* and *genesis* meaning the coming to be of an individual being or person. Ontogeny then is an unfamiliar word for saying more succinctly that the subject of our concern is a being whose life is to grow and whose growth is gradual.

The newborn human infant, unlike the newborn of other higher mammals, comes into the world largely underadapted to the variegated environment of the human world. Other newborn animals have highly developed instinctual structures which provide an immediate orientation toward what is safe and useful for nourishment, security, and community. By contrast, the human infant needs a complex initiation into the values of the human world. It is for this reason that the human species has such a long childhood period. Erikson explains that this period of childhood is a period of growth through "ritualization." Although his meaning of the word ritualization is not exactly parallel with our understanding of sacred rites and rituals, what he has to say about ritual and ritualization will be very insightful for understanding how and why the high rituals of religious celebration can range between energizing power and palling boredom.[23]

Three elements seem to express the aspects of what Erikson means by ritualization: repetition, relation, and reasons. Repetition is an important part of ritualization as it functions to initiate the infant into practices which are standard behavior, necessary for adaptation to human functions, and useful for the building up of complex habits for work and communication. Repetition is an essential quality of ritual, whether in the framework of personal growth (ontogeny) or in the context of sacred rites. A firmly rooted sensorimotor habit is an action which has, with practice, become "second nature." Such behavior as heading for a toilet for the relief of one's bladder or using table utensils with ease when eating illustrates the effects of repetition in early human learning. Because of adult insistence, children learn to take for granted social rituals of manners and cooperation. As in the development of any habit, ritual is repetitive precisely in order to root deeply an orientation which can be drawn upon at a moment's notice, even unconsciously.

Another aspect of ritualization for Erikson is its relational quality. Rituals take place between persons who are vitally involved with one another. The quality of their relationship has everything to do with the feeling tone and effect of the ritual process. Ritual binds persons together as well as develops interactions which establish a world of shared meanings. The relational aspect of ritualization maintains meaning even when the individual is threatened by sickness or separation. Social meanings are shared meanings, shored up by familiarity and convention, even when one may find little or no satisfaction in maintaining the convention. Meanings become "objectivated" by being shared, as Peter Berger explains, and through objectification they resist an individual's skepticism or loss of heart.[24]

The third aspect of ritualization is that it provides reasons. Because ritual is relational, it is always a sharing of meaning. Usually, as Erikson explains, it is intergenerational in structure: the mother interacting with the infant; parents interacting with the toddler; the family interacting with the play age child; and teachers and others interacting with the school-aged child. Reasons are provided in human growth not only by some process of telling, reading, or instruction. Reasons are more properly constructed as an individual's response to the taken for granted values of those more skilled and more creative around us.

The small child delights in sharing the activities of more skilled adults, its reward being merely the satisfaction of sociality. Children enjoy taking part in the social life of attractive others to whom they belong. They do things long before they understand fully. The "reasons for things" exist in someone else's understanding. To move toward full understanding is to become a bearer of reasons. Once again, the ritualization process is the context. It is through trying on meanings we see in others' behavior that we arrive at satisfactory meanings for ourselves. Most reasons are taken in unselfconsciously in this manner, as children adjust themselves to a comfortable place within the actions and reactions of the group to which they belong.

Play in the child's life most clearly illustrates the dynamics of repetition, relation, and reasons as elements of growth through a framework of ritualization. The sensory life of the infant takes in more information than the child's motor apparatus has the capacity to use. This results in a prolonged period of "scanning the environment" without a full capacity to respond through appropriate activity. This creates an imaginative space where the raw materials for human meaning repose in the memory and imagination of the child long before clear meanings do.

But, as Suzanne Langer comments, in the human person impulses must play themselves out. Play, like dreaming, is an activity where sensory stimuli have scope both to play themselves out as well as to discover, tentatively and gradually, appropriate meanings.[25] According to this understanding play will be an activity psychically appropriate for the whole life span of the human person including adulthood. For the fully alive adult is someone who, though to a lesser degree than children, scans the environment, taking in more stimulation than can be dealt with immediately. Even adults seek fuller meanings. As we will argue later, adults who do not know the playful nature of ritual and ritualization—the exploratory range of deep, questing interactions within the formal structure of repeated rites—will become dead to the enlivening potential of their cosmic surroundings as well as thoroughly bored with the ritual dynamics of their community. For these reasons it will be important to keep in mind how fluid a notion play is for Erikson and how integrally it functions in the elaboration of his theory of the "ontogeny of ritualization."

DEVELOPMENT IN THE FRAMEWORK OF RITUALIZATION

For Erikson the developmental agenda of the infant and child growing into the youth and adult becomes the source for the structuring of ritualization. Each child becomes familiar by ritualization with a particular version of human existence. The child thus develops a distinct sense of corporate identity—belonging to a family, an ethnic group, a culture, and other groups with social meaning.

The general design of Erikson's life cycle can be briefly summarized. In each stage of life, beginning with the newborn infant, a particular agenda of development appears which corresponds to the processes of biological maturation and social interaction. The newborn infant, totally dependent for life, nurture, and security upon others, lives between the dialectic of trust and mistrust. Healthy development leads to the virtue of hope. As the older infant begins to crawl and later walk, there is a tension between autonomy (getting around on one's own, developing increased capacity to become independent) and the strong lingering dependency needs normal to a small child. The issues of holding on or letting go provide the developmental context for the virtue of will.

At the age of four or five years old, the "play age," the key developmental issue is the modelling power of mother and father as types for imitation. Through often embarassing incidents play age children discover that they do not have either the understanding or the skill to keep up with the adult activities of parents, even though at this time these parents are for the first time consciously "love objects" for the children. Fortunately at this time healthy children increasingly develop peer interaction, providing activities which allow for the free co-construction of meanings appropriate to the culture they share with other young children. The developmental achievement of this complex period is known as purpose. Next in the "school age" the child is confronted by a plurality of tasks consciously intended to initiate growing children into the reasons and meanings of their culture. This is a time for "making things" and "making things hold together." The ego strength or achievement of this period is called competence.

Later cycles continue the developmental scheme of Erikson, although these first four stages of the life cycle are central to our discussion. The identity crisis is experienced as the challenge of adolescence and the generativity crisis as the challenge of adulthood. Both of these phases of human growth will offer sources for meaningful ritualization too.

Erikson argues that the work of human development occurs in a ritual framework. In *Toys and Reasons* his focus is on everyday meaning. Yet Erikson says, "although daily custom creates ritual needs . . . [these] find periodical fulfillment in grand rituals."[26] The ritualization framework offers a picture of the foundational stuff out of which ritual symbols and religious rituals are fabricated. The qualities of ritual change as development occurs. Little by little the components of adult readiness for ritual are acquired.

The most dynamic insight of Erikson's theory is the relational context of his ontogeny. Ritualization elevates the satisfaction of immediate personal needs into the context of communal actuality. What Freud called sublimation, Erikson calls tamed eagerness. While Freud found repression to be the most inescapable fact of human psychological life, Erikson, on the contrary, finds the need for others to be the center of gravity of human psychology.

Finally, ritual generates a shared vision, a view of reality shared by a community. This shared vision is only partly articulate and still largely tacit. Gesture, glance, touch, and presence carry a freight of meaning together with words, objects, and rules.

Particular ritual qualities are acquired in distinct phases of development in the life cycle. Those qualities impact on key symbols of the Christian life. I will take the God-image and the self-image as crucial symbols whose dynamics will depend upon the success of Erikson's ontogeny of ritualization.

The Ritual Framework for Human Growth

Erikson's first example of ritualization in everyday life is the way in which a mother and newborn infant light up when they meet one another. He gives a description of the characteristic greeting between mother and baby:

> The awakening infant awakens in the maternal person a whole repertoire of emotive, verbal, and manipulative behavior. She approaches him with smiling or worried concern, brightly or anxiously voicing some appellation, and goes into action: looking, feeling, sniffing, she discovers possible sources of discomfort and initiates services to be rendered by rearranging the infant's position, by picking him up, and so on. This daily event is highly ritualized, in that the mother seems to feel obliged, and not a little pleased, to repeat a performance arousing in the infant predictable responses, which, in turn, encourage her to proceed.[27]

This kind of ritual is highly individual in that it expresses the personality of a particular mother attuned to a particular infant. Yet it is also stereotyped along lines which can be carefully analyzed. It is both free and prescribed. The general structure of ritual interaction here is dictated by the biological or personal needs of the interacting parties.

This scene of mother and child illustrates graphically the intergenerational quality of everyday ritualization. The infant brings to this meeting vital needs, among them oral, sensory, and tactile drives, as well as the need to have disparate experiences brought into the unity that mothering gives to infantile life. A new mother also brings needs for the realization of her instinctive sense of mothering and for whatever gratification she may seek in motherhood. These mutual needs assure the interplay which makes up the aspects of this early ritual. Among these aspects are the mutuality of recognition of a face, a voice, a smell, and a name.

According to Erikson, the human infant "is born with the need for . . . regular and mutual affirmation . . . : we know at any rate that its absence can harm an infant radically, by diminishing or extinguishing his search for impressions which will verify his senses."[28] This need for affirmation throughout the life span will demand new and formalized ritualizations which repeat the face-to-face recognition and the name-to-name correspondence between personal needs and the objects of human hope. Everyday ritualizations range from symbolic exchanges of greeting to traditional affirmations of roles through signs of bestowed honors, intimacy, or dependence. At their best such ritual meetings are a kind of paradox: "they are *playful* and yet *formalized;* quite *familiar* through repetition, they yet renew the *surprise* of recognition."[29]

In the context of the newly born, the dependent infant lives always in the shadow of a fear of separation and abandonment which needs to be compensated for by periodic affirmation. This makes of the mother's person a hallowed presence, which "contributes to mankind's ritual-making a pervasive element which is best called the *numinous.*"[30] The numinous is, of course, indispensable as a ritual quality. While all institutions draw upon the numinous evocation of splendor or wonder, organized religion has the strongest claim to being associated with the numinous or sense of the supernatural. Believers learn gestures appropriate in expressing dependence, offering, and infinite yearning. "Childlike faith . . . seeks . . . to secure the privilege of being lifted up to the very bosom of the divine. . . ."[31]

So infancy contributes a capacity for the numinous which enhances the quality of any moment of high ritual. Erikson's theory is not meant to be reductionistic, as if all there were to the numinous is a nostalgia for the moment when the needy infant searches for the affirming adult who responds with the faint smile and the inclined face. Rather, Erikson affirms that this lifelong capacity to situate oneself within the framework of dependency before the transcendent is so integral to *the human* that it appears at the very beginning of human living. As Erikson explains:

> The numinous assures us of *separateness transcended* and yet also a *distinctiveness confirmed*, and thus of the very basis of a sense of "I," renewed (as it feels) by the mutual recognition of all "I's" joined in a shared faith in one all-embracing "I Am."[32]

Erikson talks next about the ritual of early childhood and the "judicious." He explains:

> The ontological source of this second kind of ritualization is the second stage of life, characterized . . . by rapid advances in psychosocial *autonomy*. As the ability to crawl and eventually to stand serves increased self-reliance, it also soon leads to play with the boundaries of the permissible.[33]

Just as the first stage develops the rudiments of hope, so this second stage develops the basic strength called will. An important issue here is "toilet training." Autonomy includes the ability to stand upright without assistance; to crawl or walk on one's own; and to move around in a world which increasingly responds to one's own will. But autonomy also concerns the capacity to control urination and defecation. This involves a relationship with parents which will include coercion, punishment, being urged on, and being rewarded.

This new structure of demands, rules, and rewards opens up a new experience of life for the child. Erikson says, ". . . autonomy soon finds its limits in our sensitive awareness of being watched by superior persons and of being called names. . . . Worse, we are shamable, and we blush for all to see."[34] More difficult than physical coercion or corporal punishment is the child's feeling of being spied upon. Not only do mothers keep a vigilant watch upon children being toilet-trained, but they lay down enduring demands: "Don't you *ever* do that again!" Children respond to this new type of human experience by constructing within themselves what Freud called (for a somewhat later developmental stage) the superego. This is "a part of ourselves standing watch over the rest of ourselves" which blames us unconsciously, even when mother or other "watchers" are not in sight, and leads us to the feeling of guilt and the need to be punished.

Such inescapable developmental experiences explain why each of us at times feels unacceptable or unsuccessful. Furthermore, in the natural human vying for esteem, affirmation, and place within a social world, these developmental issues also explain how we come to look down on others. By-products of this stage of life tend to be self-doubt and hidden shame. This explains the "origin not only

of the *divided self* but also . . . of the *divided species.*"[35] Because
the need to excrete is a lifelong condition of the human person,
childhood experiences of disapproval of excretion in inappropriate
locations lead the person to maintain a divided sense of the self as
approved and simultaneously disapproved. Erikson calls the rituals
of this period "judicious." The discrimination of good from bad is
learned, as so much else in early human life, by imitation. The child's
patterning of values follows parental values. This developmental
issue is important, since it can lead either to legalism or to a judicious freedom.

The third stage of the life cycle for Erikson is the "play age."
Here *initiative* comes into play. This stage deals with the differentiation of the personality of the play-age child from the love object
(mother) or model figure (father). Psychoanalysis calls this the
"Oedipus complex." Erikson speaks of it this way:

> If you say that the little boy "falls in love" with his mother, and that
> later on he has trouble falling out of love with her, we must remem-
> ber that from the beginning she was everything to the child. She was
> his first love "object" . . . . The problem is that the mother becomes
> "naturally" involved in the boy's first genital fantasies, at a time when
> his whole initiative has to be and is ready to be deflected from the
> home and must find new goals. Immense new faculties develop in him
> at this time, and if his potentialities are permitted to develop fully,
> the child will be in much less danger of developing a severe complex.[36]

The Oedipal situation raises the question of goal-directedness. These
descriptions, following Erikson, express patterns more characteristic
of male rather than female development. The Oedipal issue for
women is still a matter of great dispute. Nonetheless, the general
drift of cognitive and social development for boys and girls will
be very similar even here. As growing children are forced to become less dependent upon their mothers, they need to identify with
people whose work and personality they can understand and appreciate.

Erikson's notion of "purpose" here entails a lot of new achievements. Children at play are not just posing their will against
another's or practicing their ability to manipulate. At this point children begin to have projects. They learn to think in images and meanings. The use of toys, peer play, and the development in imagination
of domestic scenarios create for the child ". . . a micro-reality . . .
in order to relive, correct, and re-create past experiences, and anticipate future roles and events with the spontaneity and repetitive-
ness which characterize all creative ritualization."[37] Children at play

deal with a wide range of activity. They try to understand what leads to happiness and what leads to guilt. Though they are still largely controlled by their parents' injunctions, children through play are able both to explore reality as adults see it and to devise attractive fantasy-laden alternatives.

As the mother becomes less the "love object," the father becomes more the "model figure." Through imitation the child patterns behavior upon the example of the same sex parent. Through both spoken and unspoken, conscious and unconscious influences, both parents influence the child in developing a positive sense of an ideal self. "Psychoanalysis calls [this] the *ego-ideal*—that part of ourselves which we can look up to, at least insofar as we can imagine ourselves as ideal actors in an ideal plot, with the appropriate punishment and exclusion of those who do not make the grade."[38] The ego-ideal becomes just as internalized as any other aspect of psychological reality, exercising its own demands for certain social and personal qualities. Since, however, children's aspirations for life roles outstrip their capacities, there is much room for fantasy in their exploration of the future. Here the child comes to interplay through imagination with the fantasy world of fairy tales and picture books, myths and stories, traditions and sacred rituals. Saints and heroes, as well as imaginary companions, provide encouraging and consoling companionship to play-age children in their pensive moods.

Given their advances in cognitive growth and peer interaction, these children are not only *able* but also *need* to create a coherent plot from the conflicts that come out of simultaneous withdrawal from parental dependence and increasing advance into personal initiatives. Since the need here is for some cogent resolution of the conflicts of life, Erikson calls the ritual form of the play age "the dramatic." Says Erikson:

> In this development the dramatic does not replace, it joins the numinous and judicial elements, even as it must rely on the elements as yet to be traced ontogenetically: performance and commitment. Nor can any ritual, rite, or ceremony dispense with the dramatic.[39]

The fruit of the resolution of this cycle is called "purpose," the ability to place an intention which runs beyond the concrete limits of a single episode and flows into a sequence of events that carries one into a hopeful future. The child's thinking here demands a plot, a purpose, and some initial sense of proportion. Some things become central, others secondary. The child can bargain, given an orientation to chosen goals.

Around the age of six or seven, the child transforms play into work. The formerly random interplay of children with peers and parents in the play age becomes highly ritualized in school. Prescribed tasks are taught as basic techniques for participation in the technical world which is the child's culture. The key aspect of this phase is "method." Children are segregated into a uniform peer culture as "students," and their competition with one another becomes an important focus of social development.

The tension of the school age is the dialectic between industry and inferiority. Industry here means success at appropriating the techniques of the culture, from right spelling and writing to right thinking and valuing. The other pole of the tension at this age of development Erikson describes as inferiority, as "not being able to live up to the demands of physical performance and mental discipline required for the basic techniques taught."[40] Inferiority leads to the danger of overformalization, perfectionism, or empty ceremonialism. In any case the enduring element for the ritual life is the "formal" quality of behavior and interaction. Erikson calls the successful development of this stage "competence," self-possession based upon one's conviction of being able to get things done.

All these elements—numinous, judicial, dramatic, and formal—together form a common potentiality to realize the power of symbol within ritual interaction. Symbols have the power to formulate experience, evoke urgency, summon an assembly, claim meaning, and situate shared experience. They do this because beyond touching the "formal" elements of traditional rites, they touch as well the "dramatic" aspect of significant purpose, the "judicial" aspect of affirming a shared understanding of good and bad, as well as the most basic "numinous" aspect of wonder and dependency. These qualities endure as capacities of adult ritual life.

Our sense of wonder and anticipation (the numinous) will still be evoked by the ritual of personal greeting, with the implication that impersonal groupings of persons at liturgy will be experienced as the adult counterpart of infants unsure of their identity and lost in an undecipherable surrounding. Our feelings of approval and empowerment will depend upon the judicial element which is able to make connections between liturgy and life. Our sense of joy and purpose in religious living will continue to be influenced by the joyful or compulsive quality of leadership models, leading on the one hand to an integration of religion with everything we do and on the other to scrupulosity or fear. Our sense of formal rituals will result in either a satisfying world of personal self-investment or a flat, boring world of arbitrary demands, depending upon the way these elements come together. Part of the story of our liturgical experience has to do with the resonance which our present celebrations strike in the religious psyche of those who celebrate.

ADOLESCENCE AND ADULTHOOD

While the formal, the dramatic, the judicial, and the numinous are the core of Erikson's understanding of the epigenesis of adult ritual, there remain two further qualities pertaining to the adolescent and adult. Erikson has become known for his lucid description of the identity crisis. At the end of childhood, growing young adults come to have a distinct sense of themselves based on what they themselves repeatedly judge to be valuable, apart from the preferences or ideas of parents, teachers, and peers. Of course adolescents have peer support in distancing themselves from parental demands and the formal expectations of schools, bosses, and the culture at large. But the identity problem arises from the confusion caused by the various ways in which the same young person finds himself or herself perceived by significant adults. Such a situation breeds a need to choose for oneself the values and goals which allow one a sense of "individual self" and an "ideological identification."

Adult reactions promote a strange cognitive world where young people appear to themselves more clear and more committed than their elders. This is the classic situation within which "idealism" breeds. In calling this idealism "ideology," Erikson means a highly personalistic set of ideals which represent young persons' disaffection with available social reality and their impatience to bring about a utopian situation. In such a stance young people are enormously vulnerable to fake ideas. Yet they are likewise endowed with enormous energy and loyalty for newly conceived ideals. Erikson calls the ritual element in this context *totalism:* "that is, a fanatic and exclusive preoccupation with what seems unquestionably ideal within a tight system of ideas."[41] The fruit of all this psychic toil is called "ideological commitment." What Erikson calls commitment here he elsewhere calls fidelity. Fidelity means the total self-involvement of the individual young person in personal convictions (ideology). But it also means, significantly, a "solidarity of conviction." This solidarity is a togetherness of young people sharing in a tentative co-construction of a political and spiritual world. This adds an affiliative element to ritual. Without this sense of belonging, neither the urgency nor the energy necessary for a sustained involvement in the ideals of the human community could long endure.

Finally the ritual framework of human growth is expressed in adult graduation rituals. These may be the passage of adults to professions, marriage and parenting, or roles of authority. In any case these rituals echo and reaffirm the ritualizations of childhood. The investiture of an individual with ritualized authority, through a professional role or political leadership, helps to bind the culture into a unity.

Erikson calls such a passage into an authority role "ritual sanction." Adult rites express the "generational" power of an office. These include parenting, teaching, mentoring, healing, promoting, reassuring, and legitimating. "Tradition rituals" of one sort or another exist for each of these adult authority functions, which brings us back to ritual (and sacred rituals) at the end of this detour on the "ontogeny of ritualization." In Erikson's words:

> We can see . . . what rituals must accomplish: by combining and renewing the ritualizations of childhood and affirming generative sanction, they help to consolidate adult life once its commitments and investments have led to the creation of new persons and to the production of new things and ideas.[42]

Each ritual aspect provides a basic element for the adult ritual of societies: faith in a cosmic order, a sense of law and justice, a hierarchy of ideal and evil roles, and the fundamentals of technology, along with ideological perspectives.

Symbolic and Diabolic Orientations in God-Imagery

COMING TO VALUE THE SUBJECT IN LITURGICAL THEOLOGY

A twenty-three-year-old graduate student told me that all religion does is spoil our fun. The churches tell us that God wants us to kowtow before ridiculously limited rules. Who needs this? He was not far from Karl Marx's critique of religion as uninterested in our individual strengths and interested only in irrelevant, socially alienating rituals. Such thinking surely will effect a person's readiness for ritual.

Theologians may sometimes give the impression that one could adequately deal with liturgical theology without particular attention to the worshipping subject. A discussion of history and tradition, texts and their implications, the theological interpretation of sacramental signs, or ideal notions of community worship may be unrelated to the dispositions of the participants. To the degree that this is true, one is attempting to do a liturgical theology *without a subject.*

The notion of readiness implies that participating subjects need to be disposed to appreciate the signs, actions, and sharing of worship. This includes a readiness to relate themselves to the meaning of the texts, traditions, and actions that make up liturgy. The human subject, as a growing, changing, and dynamic person, needs to be brought into the picture of what worship really is.

Human knowing is not a "consumer activity." Pieces of knowledge are not commodities to be collected in a mental basket. Knowing is constructed within frames of reference referring to the history, relationships, and interests of living and changing persons. These frames of reference are indicated in speaking of the "magical world of the child," or the "matter-of-fact world of the adult," or later the "mystery-laden world of the aging believer." In the section which follows, I will explore one of the ways in which these differences in frame of reference lead to distinct constructions of life's meanings.

One consequence of persons' changing dispositions and frames of reference is that the same facts and ideas which church teaching or scientific writing preserves as stable entities become different constructions for persons at different levels of development. Objective ideas and facts need to be bound together with the personal story, personal meaning, and moral interests of individual persons as they live their way into the Christian mystery. The psychic space where this binding up takes place can be called the moral imagination. Moreover, ritual action is one of the principal stimuli to the moral imagination as well as the privileged forum where the moral imagination expresses itself visibly in shared meanings.[43]

Ritual action brings together and mediates *imagery* and *social meaning.* I explained above in what manner ritual symbols are archaic, complex, and many-dimensioned. Ritual symbols draw from obvious, matter-of-fact resources like texts and rubrics. But they draw also from the symbolic environment as well as from the unconscious. When a community in a context of theological faith expresses its hopes and shared visions in ritual action, their symbols mediate; they bring together many dimensions of reality to become the satisfying, shared mystery of a believing people. This is true even when some of the people scarcely dare to believe or are hesitant or inarticulate in their faith. The communal celebration of a group at a visible level embodies the needs of individual participants at a tacit implicit level.

On the other hand, ritual action is vulnerable to the unconscious influences of the changing personal-symbolic world of those who participate. For example, we are not surprised that different participants in the same liturgical celebration participate in various ways. At the same Eucharist some tell their beads, others are carried away in contemplative silence, some become involved in ritual service within the celebration, while still others read, play, sing, dance, and express in yet other ways their understanding and their investment in what is happening. Though each individual participates in common action, each one has a distinct construction of its meaning.

There are many ways in which differences of symbolic meaning might be explained. The focus here is upon the changing meaning and feeling tone of the dominant symbols which are the God-image and the self-image.

AMBIVALENCE IN GOD-IMAGERY

Too many contemporary Christians have "constructed" their theology as follows: God created the universe; God gave us the commandments to spoil all the fun; God sent his Son to make us feel guilty. Adults held captive within such a theology, not surprisingly, dismiss it as intolerable, leaving aside further exploration of whether it be true or untrue. This is diabolic (disconnected) God-imagery. One way to get at the seeds of such an inappropriate adult theology is to explore the psychological influences upon God-imagery which are raised by Erikson's explorations of ritual in ordinary life.

Christian ritual forms are controlled in part by subjective symbols. A key symbol for liturgy is God-imagery. Since ritual is a mediation of meaning, it brings together meanings from the past with the present. Ritual, however, also has the capacity to summon forth from individuals, who may have inadequate notions of God, more adequate and satisfying expressions of the relation between God and the self.

Erikson interprets life as a task not only to be mastered but also to be creatively reinterpreted.[44] A spiritual task of adulthood is to free our minds of inadequate images which control our self-understanding and our relationships. The adult imaginative capacity for rumination upon the meanings of past symbols and values allows persons to synthesize the present with the past and the future. This allows an escape from rigid, defeating images of the self and of God which can lead to self-hatred and a closed world. Too often adults, hoping to master some measure of self-respect, end up dismissing God and religion as an intolerable burden for serious adult living.

Each new stage in the life cycle offers potential for a new picture of freedom and accountability. There is a two-way cycle of responsibility. The child is responsible for responding to human overtures of greeting and invitation. The adult is responsible for "re-presenting" the values of the culture. Adults "re-presenting" cultural values also renew values insofar as each adult brings something original to the style of speaking up for the culture. Both aspects of responsibility, the child's and the adult's, lead to social health, the self-actualizing of the community.

Using the language elaborated earlier, I will call ritual exchange symbolic when it succeeds in bringing together for an individual a satisfying union with the community's traditions, the adult generation, the hopes and goals which are celebrated, and with a peer group of others who share a common frame of reference and become companions on the road to meaning. By contrast, ritual exchange can be called diabolic when these connections fail to come together. When the individual life and values of a growing young person appear alien to the community's traditions and values; when the vision of the youth does not connect with the vision of the community's adults; when the aspirations of the youth group seem foreclosed by the adults' values, then ritual symbols divide rather than unite the community. This failure can happen in liturgical celebration proper. Young people often cannot connect themselves aesthetically to "high church" music and manners. Older members of the community can cut themselves off from a "folk" style—and cut themselves off from their young as well. This failure can also emerge from ministers' and parents' lack of any real interest in youth culture. Difficult as this often is, young people need to be known through their identifying symbols and enthusiasms if they are to be realistically included within the adult community. Without this, their hopes are dashed and ritual symbols function "diabolically."

Resources for characterizing God-imagery appear at each of the life cycle stages. At each stage there is a dialectic between a denying and unsatisfying image of God and an affirming and nurturing image of God. This, by the way, respects Erikson's psychological theory. In *Insight and Responsibility* he sees the developmental achievement of each stage not as an affirmation of only positive traits and attitudes but as a realistic exploration of the full emotive and psychic scope of each stage. Thus children who develop adequately do not end up with a determinism toward unfailing trust and hope in every situation but rather an ability to respond in a way appropriate to the real situation in which they find themselves. There is a dialectic at every point in the moral and psychological life of a human person.[45]

Symbolic competence in religious understanding will involve two tasks then. The first task is to discard inadequate images of God unconsciously generated in childhood. These inadequate images can be called diabolic because, as we will see, they tend to generate a gap between human needs and the understanding of God. The second task is to replace these poor images with more appropriate ones representative of religious maturation. The first task, discarding inadequate images, is possible only in the context of the second. Ideas of God as a Tyrant—arbitrary, ungenerous, demanding—which derive from early experiences of undue childhood constraint will only dissipate as someone comes to know moving feelings of forgiveness and acceptance. Very often this occurs in spiritual direction, where someone has been impelled by a hunger for God to explore the hurts of the past. But the same exchange of feelings and imagery can erupt out of response to a sermon or a particularly beautiful Mass. In the section which follows, each stage of the life cycle is shown to have a potential for giving rise to both diabolic and symbolic content for God imagery and ritual action.

Ontogeny of Symbolic Competence

Most of the research on God-imagery now available underscores the powerful influence of parental relations with the growing child in the formation of images of God. The work of both Antoine Vergote and Ana-Maria Rizzuto indicates that mothers and fathers greatly influence their children's ideas of God. Empirical research, however, tends to leave us with very general conclusions. For example the maternal influence generates a sense of security and supportiveness, while paternal influence generates a sense of order, law, and authority.[46] Erikson's work supports this general research finding. But his theory of ritualization provides more specific focus for the theological interpretation of God-imagery. This represents an invaluable contribution to research on religious imagination.

Since it is a task of adult religion to review and readjust child-hood imagery, this present exploration will explain how adult learning resituates God-imagery in a broader context of life-span learning. In *Toys and Reasons* Erikson speaks of the need for adult reritualization. In the present context the question is perhaps better called "reimagination." I proceed stage by stage.

Infancy

The dependency of the infant upon the mother to nourish, stimulate, and reassure is the issue. The "too little too late" experience is, of course, something which every child experiences at one point or another. Every mother has other things to do than simply pay twenty-four-hour attention to her infant. What is at stake is whether a person's inner mood will be more characteristically trustful or mistrustful. John J. Gleason, Jr., goes so far as to say:

> I . . . postulate that at roughly this same developmental moment the mother or mother substitute is in a phenomenological, practical sense the child's first god . . . and that, therefore, it is at this time that every child learns his or her first unconscious, feeling-level lesson about the nature and attributes of as yet undifferentiated gods, god, God.[47]

When the baby cries out, the response of the mother is in this context a global reassurance that life as such is trustworthy.

The denying moments in infantile experience give rise to the image of God as a "Reluctant Giver." This is a summary way of estimating the feeling tone of having to wait too long for assistance, receiving only partial attention, or feeling only incomplete satisfaction with what is offered. It is hard to imagine that any child could live the full period of infancy without occasional moments where this negative attitude is the shape of his or her experience. Such God-imagery becomes "gut level" learning. Somatically situated learning lasts for a lifetime, if not corrected by more mature attitudes capable of interpreting the child's ambiguous life situation.

Infantile learning about God does come in contact with later information and experience. Wonder before the beauty and richness of the world leads to one part of an adult expansion of God-imagery. Positive experiences provide a new and richer image of God as "Unimaginable Abundance." This is the fruit of adult religious experience, which captures moments of cosmic beauty or emotive fullness and translates them into symbols of the origin of life itself.

The numinous quality is expressive of the mysterious dimensions of the world. Its opposite would be seeing the world as flat,

uninteresting, or boring. The natural religious sense of a vital adult
finds its roots in this first stage of the life cycle. On the other hand,
adults who find religion essentially boring or irrelevant may be
responding to more than simply the unsatisfactory ritual act of their
parish church. They may be responding as well to a deep-rooted,
unconscious sense that life at its deepest is flat, predictable, and
going nowhere—hopeless. Michael Cowan's chapter in this volume
further explains this loss of a sense of the numinous by pointing
out that our culture has lost enriching patterns of celebration through
its headlong rush toward efficient production at the price of true
humanity.

Here, as elsewhere, symbolic competence will entail exploring
the full scope of God-imagery from the negative to the positive.
Adults will know the dialectic of moving between the image of God
as "Reluctant Giver" and as "Unimaginable Abundance." The first
of these images can be called a diabolical orientation, since such
imagery is likely to sever ordinary reality from a fulfilling experience
of God. The latter can be called a symbolic orientation, since it situates the experience of God within our changing life experience. Ideally lightsome imagery which comes from positive adult learning will
come to illuminate the darker moments. Cardinal Newman used
to pray, "Lord, do not let me deny in the darkness what I have seen
in the light." Newman's words are an apt formula for symbolic competence for an adult, dealing with issues deriving from the first stage
of the life cycle.

Early Childhood

The issue of the second stage is autonomy. This stage decides
the ratio between cooperation and willfulness and between love and
hate that will characterize later life. Every child will, however, have
to struggle to arrive at a judicious capacity. Repetition, some failures,
some success, all lead to the ambiguous but dominant achievement
of a development of will.

The negative God-imagery of this stage is that of the "Demanding Tyrant" who insistently repeats at every moment of failure the
categorical obligation to do it right. Here the child first experiences
moral injunctions and characteristically it is a time of "Thou shalt
nots." Here is where children come to experience their own worth
as individuals independently of their deeds and misdeeds. The diabolic orientation of God-imagery at this stage will be a superego
God who is a nay-sayer. It will require adult learning of forgive-

ness to establish a dialectical experience of God as one more accepting of us than we are of ourselves.

Within this stage the beginnings of morality appear. A negative orientation in this phase will lead to an undiscerning personality. A positive and symbolic orientation will choose to seek the spirit of any law as more important than legal codes and their demands.

The values imbued by parents at this time become deeply imbedded in an emotional and prerational stratum of the personality. Such values are later modified only with great difficulty. If children experience themselves as watched, badgered, or blamed, an adult capacity for the creative discovery of values in unforeseen situations will be highly diminished. If, however, the children experience a world where, despite momentary failures and lapses in control, they are affirmed as belonging to a loving community, then the symbolic orientation to the personality may find full range with growth. Symbolic competence here entails being able to see God as naysayer as a caricature of the Reality which affirms us in the loving gift of life from day-to-day.

Play Age

There is a shift from the previous stage, in which children do not quite know what they want or why, to the developmental focus of this stage, which is purpose. Children here learn to give direction and focus to thinking and action. The child takes the voices and values of adults and makes of them an inner voice. When the child goes against the direction of that inner voice, a sense of guilt arises which is both a self-condemnation as well as parental surveillance. Such moments lead to the formation of an image of the parent-god as a "Rival God" in competition with our best efforts. At this stage children develop a new capacity for initiative. Like Oedipus the child very often feels a sense of guilt even when there is no full understanding of what is wrong, unacceptable, or problematic about a moment of life. The superego is essentially irrational, driving the child sometimes to an obedience more exacting and literal than parents desire to impose. A repressive superego can lead the child to a sense of anonymity, in which the child fails to feel like a "person" and becomes simply an automaton of others' will.

A good adult experience of the Christian life can offer another image, healing and empowering, which can stand in opposition to the notion of a "Rival God." The adult Christian may experience God who prophesies through our growth and achievements, making himself present and creative in the spontaneous initiatives of his autonomous creatures. In the teachings of the Second Vatican Council, the Constitution on the Church insists in paragraphs ten to fourteen that each of the baptized receives a charism to express in ordinary routines of life a particularized expression of the presence of God's Holy Spirit.[48] The dramatic range of ritualization, following Erikson's clues, swings from a diabolic perception of a "Rival God" who disheartens us by always outstripping the scope of our human action, to, on the other hand, an "Emmanuel" God who sacramentalizes himself in the positive moments of our personal evolution as witnesses to maturity of life. The fortunate outcome of a fully developed Christian maturity will be a person who has a definite dramatic sense of meaningful roles, modelled upon joyful adults in the ecclesial community. This maturity is itself a testimony to the healthy capacity of an adult to tie one's life together into a single, meaningful story.

School Age

The school age introduces to the ritualization of ordinary experience the aspect which Erikson calls "formal." This indicates the quality of a person's performance which meets expectations, effectively achieves some products, and expresses a distinct sense of a unique person. The core of the formal aspect of ritual is its quality of explicit definition: an identifiable, organic shape; a manageable piece of reality with distinct parts; and a product which satisfies the shared anticipation of the actor and those others who provide an environment of mutual expectation. A failure in definition will lead to chaos; a failure in achieving a product will lead to low self-esteem; and a failure in understanding that the ritual event is the joint effort of persons limited by available reality will lead to perfectionism and formalism.

The formal aspect of ritual provides structure for the dramatic, judicious, and numinous. It will be an empty structure unless the dramatic contributes a personal creative goal, unless the judicious provides an invitation to participation, and unless the numinous provides an environment of mystery and anticipation. This fourth stage is decisive socially. Here the child learns to work in true cooperation with others.

The diabolic orientation of this stage leads to God-imagery that produces a notion of a "God of Unreal Expectations." This is the stage at which ontogeny becomes truly ritualized: formal arrangements in school, complex and definite techniques, and enforced participation in the scholastic system. At some point all children feel that education demands too much of them. Someone who never finds a comfortable path through complex roles and expectations may end up a driven personality. One of the most significant debates in Christian history has been over the relative merits of a work ethic and a free grace ethic. In a world like ours, characterized by the driven quality of competition, social forces may tempt any of us to think of God as demanding the impossible. On the other hand, adult Christian celebration will, when successful, propose a symbolic orientation to God-imagery. With the New Testament, Christian preaching will proclaim God offering us energy and modelling strength in Christ. Symbolic ritual signs will embody shared experiences in a context of faith which help adult Christians to own and energize their life work. Their overbusy activities are redeemed by the healing experience of God witnessing to his power and grace available in the incarnate ministry of his Son. By such insight the inevitable formal arrangements of adult professional and productive life come to be imbued with a prophetic vision of meaning deriving from the Gospel and with a realistic sense of the limits of competitive striving.

Adolescence and the Ideal

In taking their values into their own hands, youth distance themselves from others' claims on them as well as others' taken for granted support. Youths are inclined at such a moment to either "drop out" in order to gain time or to grasp at a vision of ideological perfection which offers oversimplified answers. A cause or ideology is the vehicle used to unite the numinous, the judicious, the dramatic, and the formal. Some crusade, heightened by a sense of urgency, unifies youth's interests and provides issues for peers to bond together around the cause.

In the light of this familiar scenario of adolescents, the diabolic orientation to God-imagery is that of an "Alienating God" who asks worthless acts of self-denial and unquestioned conformity. So many parents respond to their children's dropping out of Sunday worship by making a big scene, that few succeed at identifying the underlying need their children have to distance themselves from parental values, including religion. Youth caught in such a situation will project onto God the imagery of one who asks for irrelevant and to them meaningless participation in boring and formalistic rites. God comes to be identified with all those forces which tend to throw a person back into a prison of alien expectations.

On the other hand, adult theological experience and communal Christian living will provide another idea. The symbolic orientation to God-imagery in the fifth stage of the life cycle is a "God who calls us to become unique." This is the realization of Paul's theology of the Body of Christ in 1 Corinthians and Romans, a teaching of the valued uniqueness of each member.

The expressive range of God-imagery at this stage will extend through anger at a God who seems to legitimate all the most rigid and worn-out traditions of the Church to a powerfully moving sense of divine vocation. Vocation includes a recognition of one's uniqueness as a person, an affirmation of a path to self-expression, and endorsement of the idealism of the young.

Vocation engenders commitment. The commitment motif carries forward the dimensions of ritualization. Though there is a danger of separation or elitism, the moral focus of commitment is the renewal of the entire society. When youth become more eager for a fully functioning social order than their elders, the society itself has tapped into its most profound resources for self-actualization.

Young Adulthood

The love of young adulthood is a chosen, active love. In place of relations which are given, such as those of parents and family, the young adult transfers the experience of being cared for in a parental setting to a new, adult affiliation with a unique, respected other. Among the beauties of this experience, young adults find central the joy of being known as the unique, imaginatively active, urgently committed persons which they believe themselves to be. Certainly in infatuation, and even later in tested mutuality, a young couple feels—at least for a time—that they exist in a paradisal relation of joyful acceptance and revolutionary values.

In this context the ritual dimensions are the rites of courtship, marriage, and professional engagement. A diabolic orientation to the symbols and imagery of this period produces the notion of a "Devouring God" who is jealous of our human loves and absent from human intimacy. How odd and yet understandable it is that God-imagery, which owes much of its imagistic content to parental modelling, carries the suspicion of jealousy at this point in life. Of course parents have jealously guarded their children against hostile influences, shepherded them through safe structures of cultural behavior, and held close to them even as they tentatively set out on their own.

In a theological frame of reference, the symbolic orientation of God-imagery at this stage produces a "God who is the abundance of human intimacy." God is felt to be the invisible "third," the radiance going beyond the sum of gifts of those who love.[49] In moments when two human beings come together in a fated intimacy, there is an overflowing sense of fullness to the joy and hopes which these persons share. The strategic point for pastoral ministry here is the conviction, generated by good preaching and good theology, that God is not put off by our delights but gratified in gracing us with the amplitude of joy. The old saw of Irenaeus that "the glory of God is man fully alive" finds nonchauvinist expression in the recognition that "man" fully alive is "man and woman" mutually enlivening one another's joy. To use Erikson's terminology, the abundance of delight which is the fruit of such mutual sharing in intimacy becomes the motivation for a generativity that concerns itself with not only the children of one's family, but the children of the whole human family.

Maturity and Old Age

As adults develop beyond their preoccupations with their own natural families, they deal with the issues of generativity versus self-absorption and integrity versus despair. The virtues of caring and wisdom lead adults to the capacity to hand over to another generation the hard won treasures of their life's work. Integrity, as understood by Erikson, affirms the meaning of the life cycle. Though individuals must begin to absent themselves more and more from the center of the stage of human dramas, they nonetheless maintain the capacity to feel a part of human activities and to reaffirm the culture's choices.

Retirement and distancing from the center of action are painful experiences, which can be endured creatively only with deep faith in the loving environment not only of family but also of the numinous eternal. A diabolic orientation in this stage finds a "God of Routine" who demands repetition of the same old stuff over and over again. As dying friends leave one behind feeling abandoned or as failing energies force one to revise downward one's expecta-

tions of life, all the human rituals of waking, rising, meeting, doing, eating, and conversation become routine. The symbolic
orientation is to construct God-imagery of a "God who calls us always forward into his future." Adults who maintain loving relations with others who welcome hearing again and again the "story"
of Amazing Grace as lived by these aging pilgrims, are fortunate
indeed. A typical ritualization dynamic is the deference of respect
and love which the community offers to aging members who have
maintained radiance instead of ennui and whose hope for eternal
life has carried them forward in faith.

We find at every stage both diabolic and symbolic possibilities
for God-imagery and symbol formation. The symbols in our imagination of God and of the self are part of the basic stuff of high
ritual. We have seen how God-imagery can shift at each of the
stages. Very briefly, the same can be seen with respect to the image of the self at each stage.

Symbols of the Self: Shifting Imagery

For a psychologist the ego is an activity of consciousness, and
that activity is always in the process of "balancing" itself. The use
of the word self is shorthand which refers to a mystery beyond
description that we come to know, through the course of our life,
in various ways. Ego is the self knowing itself in a particular fashion,
influenced by feelings, social roles, and shared values. As a result
the imagery for symbols of the self also shifts according to the same
forces as the many-leveled shifts in God-imagery just explored.[50]

At the first stage the self is experienced diabolically as a
"nuisance," one whose dependent cry for assistance is met by disavowal or disinterest. On the other hand, the symbolic construct
of the self is that of "someone treasured" by the responsive mother
and the nurturing family. This construct of the self as either a
nuisance or a treasure is of course unconscious. In almost all of this
imagery of the self, the person's ego responds at such a deep level
of affirmation or denial that the dynamics of self-imagery may not
be available for reflection. Still, the adult ability to respond to the
nuisance image with later learning of oneself imaged as treasured
will enter into the dynamics of symbolic competence.

At the second stage during toilet training, the diabolic self-image
is that of an "automaton," whose only meaning is to do another's
bidding. A symbolic construct of the self develops toward a realistic and appropriate autonomy. From this comes imagery of a "dis-

tinct self," capable of will and identifying itself with its own inner movements of desire. The self at the third stage is quite similar. In the movement from maternal love object to paternal model, the diabolic construct of the self is that of an "anonymous presence," while the symbolic construct is that of a "dramatic presence." Feeling oneself part of a larger story and fitting into family yarns, ethnic traditions, and a particular sacral environment, allows children to feel secure in the various roles which allow them to think of themselves as distinctive presences.

In the fourth and fifth stages, dealing with the school age and adolescence, self-imagery is quite alike. The diabolic construct has to deal with a "floating identity," in one case not attached to any particular competence or definable set of skills, in the other case undefined by self-generated objectives. At this point the symbolic self-construct will contain a note of "destiny" which not only identifies someone with particular personal gifts, but carries as well an enthusiastic commitment to others.

In the sixth stage of intimacy, the diabolic construct of the self is of an adult "who doesn't fit in." On the other hand, "symbolically" one "categorically belongs to others." The sense of belonging, so important for a productive adult self, here mirrors the positive achievement of the first four stages of the life cycle. With intimacy one is able to find new self-acceptance in the acceptance by a beloved. One's adult capacities are affirmed and complemented by another's mutuality. In the last stages it seems clear that the self-construct needs to deal with the dilemma of the diabolic construct of one "abandoned" or the symbolic one of living in "joyful surrender."

In the preceding chapter Michael Cowan describes what he calls a transferential mode of relating to others, where one's past, rather than the present as it is, determines what a given moment of life can and cannot mean. Here is another example of what I would call a diabolic image of the self, for the transferential mode of relating is draining rather than empowering. Cowan counters this negative dynamic with the dynamics of "appreciative awareness" in which the self as person calls forth an open, receptive attitude—even to oneself—as mystery, gift, and hidden richness. His perspective also provides for a healing movement from constrictive to constructive understandings of the self.

As these dynamics of self-symbolization interact with the God-imagery variables, they produce the wide spectrum of imagination that is integral to adult religious experience. At stake are such variables as the following: a self who matters to others or who is irrelevant; a life marked by destiny or threatened by boredom; activity shared with others as inescapable drudgery or as open to playful improvisation; an experience of the world as overdefined or as awaiting creative reinterpretation; and human interaction as either a draining chore or as a vitalizing reaffirmation experience.

Both the symbol of God and the symbol of the self operate as filters through which sacred rites will be refracted to produce a particular experience of life and theology. The principal meaning given here to symbolic competence is the adult's capacity to reinterpret negative childhood experiences in terms of more positive adult experiences. Competence in this context of course entails facing up to the full scope of negative and positive. We live in both aspects of reality. But symbolic competence will at least liberate one held captive in inappropriate negative constructs of God and of the self.

As Edward Kilmartin indicates later in this volume, Christian liturgy is founded theologically upon the free initiative of God offering love and communion to believers. All considerations of readiness or of symbolic competence need to be put into that context. Development in Christian maturity has to be seen not as an achievement which merits divine favor but rather as a progressive movement into a fully functioning humanity in which alone we have the aptitude to receive and respond to God's offer of friendship and intimacy. Our response is more or less impeded by diabolic God-imagery or self-imagery. Therefore, readiness for Christian ritual takes on the character of developing a greater aptitude for encounter with God by reason of moving beyond obstacles of psychological and social incapacity.

Kilmartin rightly assigns to Jesus Christ the fully adequate or total response of humanity to God. Jesus alone manifests complete human openness to God. In consequence readiness or symbolic competence, which I account for in terms of psychological development, is seen again more as a gift than an achievement. We are able to reritualize our negative, constrictive images of God and of self because the Church holds up to us the image of Jesus Christ and the story of his attaining perfect freedom in God's grace.

The next question, then, is how to foster this adult skill of symbolic competence. By what means can the Church's ministers promote this aptitude?

Promoting Symbolic Competence

In presenting the issue of symbolic competence I have developed a number of perspectives. I began by illustrating the ambivalence of the word symbol through a dialectical set of categories called the symbolic and the diabolic. These two terms signify the *integrating* and the *alienating* dynamics of ritual signs. I used the "ontogeny of ritualization" to illustrate the step-by-step acquisition of elements integral to adult symbolic consciousness. At each step it was possible to indicate both a symbolic and diabolic functioning of symbols. Given the openness of ritual signs and of the symbols of God and self, adult psychological experience may be able to remedy inappropriate symbolization by later reinterpretation of symbols.

In the passages which follow, I will develop three further aspects of a theory of symbolic competence: the dynamic impact of modes of leadership, forms of action within the community, and theological language and its expressive range.

Styles of Community Leadership

In an interesting article which applies Erikson's theory of religious ritual to a historical case of excommunication, Donald Capps argues that religious ritual stands at the "intersection of psychological dynamics and social structures." After reviewing the ontogeny of ritualization, Capps comes to the following summary:

> In my view, each of Erikson's four types of ritual has a parallel type of religious authority: certain types of religious authority encourage certain types of ritual, and certain types of ritual encourage their corresponding authority structures. The types of authority are derived from various classifications of authority types [Wach, Weber, Eliade, and Schoeps].[51]

Each of the first four stages of the life cycle can be related to a specific style of nurture and leadership. So a plurality of elements are integral to good celebration. In any community the leader must appeal to the psychic needs of persons in a wide range of developmental stances. The average parish celebration includes the aged, mature adults, young parents, adolescents, children, and toddlers. It is fortunate that symbols characteristically have the openness which was noted above. Sometimes, even when the planned dimensions of worship are flat and narrow in scope, the power of music, sacred space, symbolic elements, and fellowship are enough to communicate with the "depths" of the participants, despite the given limitations. But to leave things there would be too self-defeating an attitude towards what we have learned. Capps offers us further clues.

A first type of leadership appeals to the numinous. The "mystic-magician" figure is someone who throws himself or herself into the ceremonial behavior: prays from the heart, preaches from experience, externalizes the transforming power of symbols through their capacity for spiritual delight, and learns mysteriously in a contemplative gaze. These forms of ceremonial behavior elicit from participants a sense of the numinous. This awe-inspiring quality of ceremony reaches both adults as well as children. Some measure of ability of this kind seems an important quality in a good leader.

Likewise the "saint-sage" figure can be dynamically described. Personal actions which affirm and include all those who participate can generate a healing sense of acceptance despite legal or cultural divisions. This type of figure creates a feeling of definiteness about the reality and the function of the religious community. Such a figure evokes more of a communion than a community, even though obviously both aspects are salient to this style of authority. A fundamental sense of law and justice and of the community's capacity to deal with such issues is generated by this style of authority.

The "prophet-reformer" figure ministers to the dramatic level of the community's ritual sense. Such a person is characterized by pragmatic good sense. It takes imagination as well as learning, compassion as well as anger to bring forward a concrete sense of a moral or a religious issue. This kind of authority brings a community to feel the urgency of its own sacral rites and of its responsibilities to the surrounding secular world. The product of the interplay of such a figure with the community will be the development among participants of clearly identified roles and a unifying sense of communal purpose.

"Pastor-teacher" figures communicate a profound sense of their identification with the community they serve. They hold in tension a two-fold objective: to promote among their charges free and autonomous competence and to insist upon the fundamentals which identify them as a community with a historic and theological tradition. The weakness of this style is its liability toward fundamentalism or formalism; its obvious strength is its ability to foster the talents and gifts of participants in the community and promote their creativity, all the while interpreting this development as continuous with the historic tradition. It is easy to see why Capps identifies this figure with the formal aspects of ritualization. This kind of authority presupposes that available forms exist to serve as vehicles for meeting present needs and future cultural development.

While research is needed to verify whether these qualities coexist in the leadership style of clearly effective church ministers, the supposition is that they do. Erikson calls this the "epigenetic" or interlocking quality of developmental achievements.[52] I believe we see this often in high-level liturgical celebration. A liturgical sense—good gestures, welcoming manner, deeply felt presence—can awaken awe. Good preaching can heal, unify, and guide action by being realistic about life and clear about the Gospel. It is rare, but sometimes we do run across a celebrant who is a combination magician, judge, prophet, and shepherd. And when we do, we realize that such a person is pulling the community together with special force. Capps argues that this happens precisely because this celebrant appeals to all the fundamental ritual elements by exercising a full range of authority.

In passing it may be important to observe that the Christian churches seem to be moving into a new period where their communities' celebrations will be marked increasingly by the interplay of many leadership roles in worship. Instead of thinking exclusively of different styles of a single clerical leader, perhaps we will have to think of various persons in the community exercising these different symbolic functions.

There are only four levels of ritual and authority correlations in Capps' work. The later stages of the life cycle depend less upon the nurture of leadership than the initiative of an autonomous personality. Adult celebration always has the nature of reritualization, the reworking of God-imagery and self-imagery within the healing context of divine forgiveness, empowerment, and transcendent promises. An important function of adult life, achieved through religious ritualization, is to rework and draw upon the strengths first generated in infancy, early childhood, and youth. This dimension of reality, though a footnote to liturgical theology, is central to the perspective of religious psychology.

COMMUNITY ACTION WHICH FOCUSES RELIGIOUS TRUTH

Since Erikson has related the four qualities of ritual (namely the numinous, the judicial, the dramatic, and the formal) to the developmental agenda of specific stages in the life cycle, it is possible to draw out further implications for the community's action in high ritual celebration. At each stage, then, I will indicate symbolic and diabolic actions which refer to the specific needs of the ritual aspects.

The numinous, generated in infancy and affirmed by the mystic-magician figure, is a quality of cognitive experience which values the poetic, respects the inarticulable horizon of religious experience, and rests in satisfaction and heartfelt fullness (which William James called "the oceanic feeling").[53] Symbolic action which supports and fosters the numinous includes the sharing of silence and respect for nonverbal communication. Teaching a community the difference between empty silences (merely waiting around) and filled-up silence (awed respect before the fullness of mystery) seems to be one of the principal ways to encourage numinous awareness among adults. The artful use of nonverbal ritual signs, such as incense, lamps, and music, also underlines the numinous. By contrast, the diabolic actions which discourage a numinous sensibility are ceremonials which become overburdened with verbalism or verbosity. (It does seem to be a problem nowadays that Christian celebrations propose to "explain everything." Too many words can paralyze communication just as surely as no words at all.)

The judicious refers to definite limits of the acceptable and the unacceptable as well as the recognition of individuals as distinct and worthy beings. A symbolic communal action is one which empowers and affirms participants, calling them to recognize themselves within the kingdom of God. On the other hand, a diabolic action elicits guilt and shame. Preaching which is inclined to blame ironically does not utilize the psychological dynamics for coconstructing with participants a manageable world with definite boundaries, but rather invites them out of the process of world-building and out of the gospel collaboration for a "New Creation."

The dramatic aspect of ritual provides participants with a meaningful sense of roles and a determinate program of objectives. Here the symbolic orientation for the community's action provides a workable story and meaningful roles, for all, rather than just the hierarchical leaders. The diabolic orientation of ritual action develops a story form with no meaningful roles for the participants. The result is ritual action which is either unfocused or boring—or both.

The formal aspect of ritual defines the parameters of shared experience and action. The symbolic formal aspect will constantly be expanding its imagination to employ the competences of talented people. Certainly, the notion of an American community's concerted action today will be very different from that of a hundred years ago. Then the community focused upon the survival of an immigrant community in a hostile environment. Today the celebrant or leader of the community is very often the conductor in an abundant symphony of talent in a wide-ranging community of professionals, skilled adults, and enthusiastic youth. The diabolic orientation of formal ritual would deny the complex talents and interests of this precise community of persons. In consequence the diabolic orientation leads to an experience of ritual action as irrelevant, unrealistic, and boring.

Justification for these suggestions, of course, depends upon the development of the "ontogeny of ritualization" argument presented above. This list of suggestions may serve best as an agenda for constant reexamination of a community's liturgical performance. In some places it may serve even better as an agenda for exploring dynamics not yet customary within the culture of the particular parish or community.

The Ambivalence of Theological Language

Erikson uses the term reritualization to express the moment when persons in adulthood begin to rework their symbols of God and of the self. This is a process which leads to personally defined or reconceived meanings for childhood imagery and ideas. It is not surprising that theological language itself undergoes such a process of meaning transformation. I am reinterpreting the reritualization theory of Erikson within the general categories of the heteronomous and the autonomous as used by developmental psychology. Heteronomy is a time in life when one is necessarily dependent upon other people's understanding and meanings. The first four stages of the ontogeny of ritualization are characterized by heteronomy.[54] Cognitive-developmental theory in general helps us to see that God-imagery will characteristically express heteronomous notions of the divine which include punishment, blame, bargaining, approval, and law and order. Only later, with the development of autonomous reasoning, does the full scope of theological meaning become integrated into the early childhood religious imagery.[55]

In this present exploration I use the notion of autonomy to represent something of Erikson's idea of reritualization. When in adulthood persons rework their symbols of God and the self, they bring autonomous meanings to the theological language they learned earlier in life. The ambiguity of some of the most fundamental theological and religious language derives from its relationship to heteronomous or autonomous attitudes. Autonomous constructions of theological ideas will have symbolic dynamics in the ritual development of persons and of communities. In parallel fashion heteronomous meanings will underline and enforce diabolic ritual experience.

The terms upon which I will remark here are the following: God, sin, holiness, prayer and contemplation, forgiveness, obedience, and tradition. In each one of these, it is possible to discern either integrating or alienating dynamics. This is one more way to explore both the symbolic and diabolic orientations of ritual symbols, as well as the general issue of fostering symbolic competence.[56]

The term God is ambivalent. Early childhood thinking generates heteronomous significations for God. Even many adult terms taken to be synonymous with God are distancing or alienating, for example, Supreme Being, the Great Architect, or the Eternal Lawgiver. Each of these synonyms associates the idea of God with a concrete world of known objects or experience, conceptually placing God as "an object among the objects of the universe." Negative theology may translate this into a phrase such as *"like this, but infinitely better,"* but, even so, the frame of reference remains the infinitely better within a set of known experience.

Yet, in fact, we do not perceive God that way. God is never discovered like an object. The expectation that God should be available as present-but-separate instead of copresent-and-immanent ends up frustrating our hunger for God or distorting it into superstition or idolatry. Liturgists have to fight against such heteronomous notions of God, which emerge in the spirituality of the "Prisoner of the Tabernacle" or the Infant Jesus of Prague and which feed a sentimental piety of escape from reality rather than a realistic piety of social presence.

Autonomous significations for God-imagery seem to follow upon meaning reversal experiences. When a timorous person suddenly experiences the transition from fear to acceptance a change occurs. At such a moment God-imagery becomes resituated as no longer something expressive of a being or force *outside* oneself but rather as the core of life itself, whose fluid boundaries will not discriminate between the self and the non-self. Contemporary theology's use of the term "Ground of Being" for God reflects this more symbolic dimension of God-imagery.

Sin and holiness are other examples of theological categories which can signify in ambivalent ways. Sin frequently functions in terms of a purely legal fundamentalism, namely, breaking a law or a code constitutes sinning. Yet mature theological understanding situates sin well beyond the merely material considerations of failing to meet expectations. Sin, linguistically related to the English word "sunder," points directly to a distancing of oneself from the presence and directive power of God; one sins when one sunders the bonds of belonging and love that give religious identity to the person. Only in this latter, nonlegalistic sense can adults finally realize the important irony that quite often moments of sin are also disguised graces, leading to a discovery of a radical need for divine encounter. The *felix culpa* (happy fault) of Adam is repeated often in the lives of those who only discover the tenderness of God's unconditional acceptance at the point that they have been reduced to extremities of loneliness and fear.

Holiness, likewise, is an ambivalent term. Heteronomous religious thought tends to identify holiness with perfect ritual observances, an idea which makes it fairly impossible for anyone to be consistently holy. St. Paul's argument in Galatians about not taking the law as the be-all and end-all of religious living is based upon the point-blank recognition that no one can successfully go through life without some ritual imperfections. But an autonomous, symbolic construction of "holiness" identifies it with *openness to God.* A diabolic orientation to holiness would make of sacral, holy things a ritual parenthesis cut off from the ordinary texture of moment-to-moment experience. By contrast, a symbolic orientation would see holiness as a transfiguration of everything, even the most lowly, into a window which gives a glimpse onto the eternal, loving source of all reality.

Prayer and contemplation, on the one hand, can be seen as human effort, offered to God in a supernatural commerce of bargaining for favors. Such a diabolic construction leaves God far off in the distance, reluctant, if not coy, in his arbitrary unresponsiveness. On the other hand, a symbolic construction of prayer and contemplation begins with the conviction that life itself, as creative empowerment and as fellowship in a community of praise, offers the incessantly repeated initiative of God inviting us into intimacy. Thus prayer becomes a response to that divine reaching out and a surrender of the self to a contemplative gaze upon the silent horizon of our active lives.

Forgiveness is similarly ambivalent. It can be seen, unfortunately, as the reluctantly given second chance, which God offers in a spirit of conditional love. Probably every Christian child at one time or other was told, "Jesus won't love you if you do that!" Adult reritualization has to rework the symbol of forgiveness to make of it a disclosure of God's loving acceptance which cannot be destroyed by human weakness. This is close to the core meaning of the story of the prodigal son. We may distance ourselves from the affirming influence of a loving father (or mother or friend), but that faithful disposition in the loving one is not eliminated by distancing ourselves. Forgiveness is discovering the enduring care which has maintained itself despite our indifference and which still possesses the capacity to bring us back to a joyful sharing of life.

Obedience, too, has similar polarities. Heteronomy tends to see obedience as meaning a disposition which makes us an automaton at another's beck and call. But the word obedience comes from a Latin etymology which means "intense listening" (*ob-audire*), and this etymology carries us into a better understanding. Obedience then signifies growing into the capacity to "hear" with the full scope of one's adult presence—including imagination, creativity, and practical wisdom—the Spirit of life. The obedience of mature Christian adults is primarily a community listening carefully for the signs of the Spirit, rather than one individual submitting to another individual. That dimension, which is a sociological reality of any complex community, exists too, but it must be given nuance by the more profound theological dimension just mentioned.

Finally, tradition is an example of another ambivalent theological category. Tradition, in a heteronomous rendering, can be the codification of the minute etiquette of a complex institution. Seen as such, it provides prefabricated norms and procedures for every conceivable activity. Tradition has come to mean a closed world for many religiously trained adults. As a consequence of this diabolic construction of its meaning, tradition is cut off from imagination, creativity, and contextual improvisation. But a symbolic construction moves in another way. Tradition can also mean the life of God with God's chosen people, transmitted as much in the silent horizons of one's moral imagination as in the articulations of texts and norms. This is not to say that there are no privileged texts or that they are unimportant. Rather, it is simply to insist on the diabolic and symbolic range of these and other concepts.

The preaching, teaching, and fellowship of the parish, the diocese, and the religious community can reinforce either a diabolic denying construction or a symbolic affirming construction of religious culture. The usage and interpretation of theological categories in a symbolic orientation by a Christian community can have sometimes dramatic impact on reflective adults, who may be thereby invited to rework their religious ideation in the wake of more positive interpretations.

It is worth noting that some understandings are not just heteronomous, but that they are erroneous or inadequate in themselves. My consideration is limited to developmental issues. Therefore, the chief message here is that all of us seem to go through a progress in theological understanding based upon the growth of our capacities for religious and social thinking. There is no doubt, however, that many adults maintain heteronomous or preadult theological understandings and that, in consequence, their capacities to learn from the wisdom of the Church community are thereby greatly diminished.

Applications to Pastoral Life

In his recent book Anscar Chupungco calls the gap between cult and culture the number one problem of contemporary liturgy.[57] People coming to worship expect a complete disjunction between the ordinary and the sacred. In my sense Christians today have been formed so as to expect a liturgy carried on with diabolic ritual dynamics.

Such a gap can be addressed by interpreting culture as ongoing creation. The key dimension of Christianity's ongoing creation is the ontogenesis of Christians. Believers are not players of static roles whose range of vision and action is the same week after week. They are rather selves in transformation and need to be addressed as such.

Cult likewise needs to be interpreted not as a changeless performance of timeless words and gestures but as a synthesis of ritual dynamics which extend across the social learnings of a lifetime. A good part of the problem, I think, is that many Christians have not yet become convinced that cult is living, expressive, and personal. This includes many priests. The "readiness-for-ritual" perspective developed here may have potential for changing the religious views of such persons.

Evangelical communities bring life into their celebrations of faith through witnessing. The altar call and the sharing of stories about God's blessings in the lives of the people exemplify this. The Roman Mass offers potential for this, to a limited degree, in the Prayer of the Faithful. But this is generally haphazard, ill-prepared, and underplayed in parish Masses. We need to keep an eye on the ritual opportunities we have in our present rites to speak up about the ordinary.

Another insight which comes out of this analysis is a deeper awareness of the complexity of adult ritual life. Adult readiness for ritual implies a bringing together of awe, order, interest, and involvement. Too many adult Christians—and too many priests— see order alone as the value of worship. The revitalization of a community's values depends upon engaging adult commitment. Parishes will have to work at making a world safe for honest enthusiasm—a word, by the way, which means "filled up with God."

The range of qualities which contribute to symbolic power in liturgy, coupled with a parallel range of types of authority, offers direction of a sort. While my point has not been to work out moment by moment directives for liturgical action, some concrete indications flow from this perspective. Priests and other liturgical ministers will have to become aware that the tools of their trade include the numinous, the judicious, the dramatic, and the formal. If they do not know about these tools, or do not know how to use them, will they do an honest job?

Most important, I think, is the centrality of the idea of "re-vision" in the readiness perspective. Erikson's term reritualization and my term reimagination both mean a kind of "re-visioning" of the meanings of life. In a way this book is telling the good news that we *can* "re-vision" our Christian experience as adults. But even more truly, we *do* "re-vision" our experience, whether we are aware of it or not. Liturgy has to be alert to this. Preaching and celebration are privileged channels which bring the ideas, images, and possibilities of such re-visioning to the always changing believers in the assembly.

I have tried to convince readers that adults characteristically rework the imagery they use in symbolizing God and the self. Symbolic competence has to do with becoming conscious of this fact. Liturgy has to assist communicants to reritualize their religious and moral imagination in productive, healing, and energizing ways. Retreats, counseling, adult education, and even preaching could productively review the range of God-imagery and self-imagery which the readiness for ritual perspective offers.

Liturgy is about calling people to conversion. The ontogeny of ritualization supports the plausibility that such conversions occur over and over in every life. But Erikson is inclined to speak of developmental "tasks," as though the fundamental dynamic in growth is facing up to a job we must do. In a Gospel community it is truer to leave behind the language of achievement and turn to the language of grace.

Grace is a strange word whose meanings include the idea of an undeserved surprise. The greatest grace is God's interruption of our self-preoccupation by revealing himself as a Father who forgives, heals, loves, and lives on in us. This grace offers us a wholeness that comes from God, who finds life in death, light in darkness, and power in weakness. The key to renewal is not going to depend upon the adequacy of human projects but upon the depth of our honesty before the enormity of our need and the totality of God's gift. We must preach the message—authentic in theology as in psychology— that we are each unfinished persons in an incomplete world. The pressure is off. What God is looking for from us is not someone else's faith, piety, story, or worship but ours.

In conclusion the most strategic remedy for diabolic constructions of liturgy is something that I do not need to provide. It already is at work. It is the ineradicable hunger for meaning and for life that resides, as a grace, in depths of every human consciousness and every human heart.

This chapter began by remarking upon the eternal hunger underlying all constructive actions. This hunger for meaning will be more or less poignant depending upon one's developmental perspective. As we have seen, at any point meaning is partly clear and partly hidden, but always uniquely constructed within the framework of a person's life and possibilities.

Christian sacraments offer a privileged symbolic environment for the human search for satisfying meaning. In Christian worship meanings arise out of the healing acceptance of Christian fellowship and out of the transcendent logic of the story of Jesus, Brother and Savior. The other authors in this volume also deal with the exploration of Christian sources of meaning. They clarify what has been mentioned here in passing, namely, that in Christian sacraments wholeness comes not as the fruit of human achievement but as the loving gift of a divine love breaking in upon our search for meaning.

That properly theological part of the story of Christian ritual life and sacraments will be more cogent in the context developed here. Paying attention to the structures of human growth pays off. It shows us that we have a natural vocation to search for wholeness and that we bring to that search a lively capacity to "re-vision" and restructure the self. Within this perspective "New Creation" becomes a theme not only of New Testament theology but of ordinary life as well.

Footnotes

1. Bernard Lonergan, "Dimensions of Meaning," *Collection* (New York: Herder and Herder, 1967) 252–269. See also Bernard Lonergan, *Method in Theology* (New York: Herder and Herder, 1972) 57–101. Susanne K. Langer, *Philosophy in a New Key* (Cambridge, Mass.: Harvard University Press, 1978) 266–294.

I am eager to express my thanks to Christopher Durney, who commented helpfully upon earlier drafts of this chapter, and to Jeff Hartling, who provided research assistance as I worked on this chapter. Ann Aubin generously typed multiple drafts of these pages. To them and others I am grateful.

2. Raymond Vaillancourt, *Toward a Renewal of Sacramental Theology*, trans. by Matthew O'Connell (Collegeville, Minn.: Liturgical Press, 1979). See also R. Kevin Seasoltz, *New Liturgy, New Laws* (Collegeville, Minn.: The Liturgical Press 1980) 38–112.

3. Aidan Kavanagh, "Life Cycle Events, Civil Ritual and the Christian," *Concilium* no. 112 (1979) 14–25. R. Kevin Seasoltz, "Anthropology and Liturgical Theology, Searching for a Compatible Methodology," *Concilium* no. 112 (1979) 3–14. James W. Fowler, "Theology and Psychology in the Study of Faith Development," *Concilium* no. 156 (1982) 87–91.

4. Peter L. Berger, *The Sacred Canopy* (New York: Doubleday, 1967) 3.

5. Hans G. Furth, "Symbol Formation: Where Freud and Piaget Meet," *Human Development* (Basel) 26, no. 1 (1983) 26–41.

6. See Lonergan, *Method in Theology* 41–47.

7. Langer, *Philosophy in a New Key* ch. 3, "The Logic of Signs and Symbols." Paul Ricoeur distinguishes between uses of symbol in psychoanalysis, poetry, and comparative religion in "Parole et symbole," *Le symbole*, ed. Jacques-E. Ménard (Strasbourg: Faculté de Théologie Catholique, 1975) 142–161.

8. Erik H. Erikson, *Insight and Responsibility* (New York: W. W. Norton, 1964) esp. 111–157. See Walter E. Conn, *Conscience: Development and Self-Transcendence* (Birmingham, Ala.: Religious Education Press, 1981) 34–105. Conn interprets the Eriksonian account of adolescent transition to adulthood as a transformative journey of the ego toward self-transcendence.

9. Lonergan, *Method in Theology* ch. 1. See Robert Doran, "Jungian Psychology and Christian Spirituality," *Review for Religious* 38 (1979) 497–510. Lonergan's terminology is "restless yearning" and "radical intending."

10. Christopher Kiesling, "Liturgy and Consumerism," *Worship* 52, no. 4 (July, 1978) 359–369.

11. See, e.g., John Crossan, *The Dark Interval: Toward a Theology of Story* (Chicago: Argus Communications, 1975); also John Crossan, *Cliffs of Fall: Paradox and Polyvalence in the Parables of Jesus* (Minneapolis: Seabury Press, 1980). Another study of the passage from myth to meaning is Raimundo Panikkar, *Myth, Faith and Hermeneutics* (New York: Paulist Press, 1979) esp. 2–16.

12. Hans Furth, "Symbol Formation," and David Tracy, *Blessed Rage for Order* (Minneapolis: Seabury Press, 1980) 32–43.

13. Jean Piaget, *Six Psychological Studies* (New York: Vintage, 1967) ch. 1. Ronald Goldman, *Religious Thinking from Childhood to Adolescence* (Minneapolis: Seabury Press, 1964) 51f.

14. James E. Loder, *The Transforming Moment: Understanding Convictional Experiences* (New York: Harper & Row, 1981) ch. 5. James W. Fowler, *Stages of Faith* (New York: Harper & Row, 1981) 24–31 and 184–198.

15. *Readings in Moral Education*, ed. Peter Scharf (Minneapolis: Winston Press, 1978) 2–75.

16. Susanne K. Langer, *Feeling and Form* (New York: Scribner's, 1953). Daniel Stevick, *Language in Worship, Reflections on a Crisis* (Minneapolis: Seabury Press, 1971).

17. See, e.g., *The Philosophy of Paul Ricoeur*, eds. Charles E. Reagan and David Stewart (Boston: Beacon Press, 1978) chs. 3 and 10 esp.

18. George S. Worgul, Jr., *From Magic to Metaphor* (New York: Paulist Press, 1980). Louis Bouyer, *Rite and Man: Natural Sacredness and Christian Liturgy* (Notre Dame, Ind.: University of Notre Dame Press, 1963).

19. Edward F. Edinger, *Ego and Archetype* (New York: Putnam, 1972). Mary Douglas, *Natural Symbols: Explorations in Cosmology* (New York: Pantheon, 1970).

20. *Music in Catholic Worship* (Washington: U.S.C.C.—Bishops' Committee on the Liturgy, 1972) 1, #6.

21. Jörg Splett, "Symbol," in *Encyclopedia of Theology*, ed. Karl Rahner (New York: Seabury, 1975) 1654–57. See Rollo May, "The Significance of Symbols," in *Symbolism in Religion and Literature*, ed. Rollo May (New York: Braziller, 1960) 11–49.

22. See "In Solidarity and Service: Reflections on the Problem of Clericalism in the Church," Publication of the Ad Hoc Task Force on Clericalism, Conference of Major Superiors of Men (Silver Spring, Md.: C.M.S.M., 1983).

23. Erik H. Erikson, *Toys and Reasons: Stages in the Ritualization of Experience* (New York: W. W. Norton, 1977). See Worgul, *From Magic to Metaphor* 52–67, for a congenial exploration of Erikson's ideas relative to ritual.

24. Berger, *The Sacred Canopy*, ch. 1.

25. Susanne K. Langer, *Mind: An Essay on Human Feeling*, Vol. 2 (Baltimore: Johns Hopkins University Press, 1972) ch. 17, esp. 288–9.

26. Erikson, *Toys and Reasons* 79.

27. *Ibid.* 85.

28. *Ibid.* 88.

29. *Ibid.*

30. *Ibid.* 89.

31. *Ibid.*

32. *Ibid.* 90.

33. *Ibid.* 92.

34. *Ibid.* 93.

35. *Ibid.* 95.

36. Richard I. Evans, *Dialogue with Erik Erikson* (New York: Dutton, 1969) 24.

37. Erikson, *Toys and Reasons* 99–100.

38. *Ibid.* 101.

39. *Ibid.*

40. *Ibid.* 105.

41. *Ibid.* 110.

42. *Ibid.* 112.

43. Craig Dykstra, *Vision and Character* (New York: Paulist Press, 1981). Dykstra considers imagination (vision) the foundation of both morality and worship; see chs. 4 and 5. See Stanley Hauerwas, *Vision & Virtue* (Notre Dame, Ind.: Fides, 1974).

44. Erikson, *Toys and Reasons* 115–145.

45. Erikson, *Insight and Responsibility* ch. 4.

46. *Toward Moral and Religious Maturity*, eds. J. W. Fowler and A. Vergote (Morristown, N.J.: Silver Burdett, 1980): Antoine Vergote, "The Dynamics of the Family and Its Social Significance for Moral and Religious Education," 89–114; Ana-Maria Rizzuto, "The Psychological Foundations of Belief in God," 115–135. Andrew M. Greeley, *The Religious Imagination* (Los Angeles: Sadlier, 1981). Antoine Vergote and Alvaro Tamayo, *The Parental Figures and the Representation of God* (The Hague: Mouton, 1981).

47. John J. Gleason, Jr., *Growing Up to God* (Nashville: Abingdon, 1975) 26.

48. See David N. Power, *Gifts That Differ: Lay Ministries Established and Unestablished* (New York: Pueblo Publishing Co., 1978).

49. Robert Johann, *The Meaning of Love* (Glen Rock, N.J.: Paulist Press, 1966). See Walter E. Conn, *Conscience: Development and Self-Transcendence* 66–79.

50. William F. Kraft, *The Search for the Holy* (Philadelphia: Westminster, 1971).

51. Donald Capps, "Erikson's Theory of Religious Ritual: The Case of the Excommunication of Ann Hibbens," *Journal for the Scientific Study of Religion* 18, no. 4 (December 1979) 348.

52. Erikson, *Insight and Responsibility* 134–141.

53. William James, *The Varieties of Religious Experience* (New York: Macmillan, 1961).

54. Jean Piaget, *The Moral Judgment of the Child* (New York: Free Press, 1969) 84–108.

55. See Ronald Duska and Mariellen Whelan, *Moral Development: A Guide to Piaget and Kohlberg* (New York: Paulist Press, 1975) 80–99.

56. A study of the ambivalence of theological and liturgical categories can be found in Christian Duquoc and J. Guichard, *Politique et vocabulaire liturgique* (Paris: Editions du Cerf, 1975).

57. Anscar J. Chupungco, *Cultural Adaptation of the Liturgy* (New York: Paulist Press, 1982).

3. THEOLOGY OF THE SACRAMENTS:
TOWARD A NEW UNDERSTANDING OF THE CHIEF RITES OF THE CHURCH OF JESUS CHRIST

Edward J. Kilmartin, S.J.

Introduction

The Roman Catholic, Byzantine Orthodox, and so-called Ancient Oriental Orthodox Churches, along with high church elements of churches stemming from the Reformation, agree on the number of principal liturgical rites which play a role in the life of faith. They are baptism, confirmation, Eucharist, reconciliation of sinners, anointing of the sick, orders, and matrimony. While a certain resemblance exists between them, this is modified by a greater dissimilarity. Baptism, for example, cannot serve the purpose of the Eucharist. Yet both relate to the one economy of salvation in a similar and ordered way. Hence, an interpretation of both must take into account the peculiarities of each, as well as their similarities.

A systematic elaboration of the meaning of each sacrament is necessary in order that Christians may gain that knowledge of the role of each in the life of faith which will enable participation according to one's level of maturity. On the other hand, it is also pastorally useful to have available a theological synthesis which concentrates on the common aspects of the seven rites, thereby developing more fully principles which are applicable to them all. Ideally such a treatise furnishes a deeper appreciation of the place of all the sacraments within the economy of salvation and, correspondingly, contributes to a better understanding of all aspects of Christian revelation.

Once theologies of individual sacraments have been sufficiently developed, the more comprehensive approach is made possible. A theology of sacraments "in general" is legitimate to the extent that it derives from reflection on the chief rites themselves. From this more comprehensive theology the notion of a chief rite of the Church emerges, which characterizes all of them intrinsically. The Western theological tradition, since the twelfth century, gives this notion the name sacrament.

During the Patristic period and the early Middle Ages the term sacrament had a much broader meaning. Moreover there was no other single word which was used in a technical and exclusive sense for the chief rites of the Church. This corresponds to the fact that no systematic theology of sacraments existed, although St. Augustine had already furnished a valuable point of departure through his penetrating analysis of the concept of sacred sign *(signum sacrum).* Systematic treatises, which enabled the formulation of the concept sacrament applicable to the chief rites, were worked out for the first time by twelfth century Scholastic theologians.

Theologians in the high Scholastic period of the thirteenth century consolidated and contributed significantly to the theology of sacraments of the previous century. Since then progress has been slow. The process of thinking through the meaning of sacrament has not always resulted in new gains, and sometimes there has been a loss of ground. But this is nothing new to the history of reflection on each and every aspect of the economy of salvation. Indeed, it is probably too much to expect that a completely satisfactory explanation of the concept of sacrament will ever be achieved. For the principle of intelligibility in Christian theology is the relationship of one aspect of the economy of salvation to all the others. Hence a systematic theology of sacraments intends to take account of all factors which make the concept sacrament understandable. However, it is difficult to imagine that any theologian or school of theology could command such a grasp of the whole of Christian revelation as to be able to formulate the definitive theology of the sacraments.

The history of theology makes it abundantly clear that each age has its own contributions to make to the understanding of the life of faith. These are conditioned by a variety of cultural and historical circumstances. In one age, with its peculiar questions provoked by a special religious experience and understanding of reality, some aspects of the theology of sacraments may be highlighted while others, which received attention previously, are neglected. A new age, stimulated by its own religious needs, may rediscover those forgotten aspects and contribute to the overall intelligibility by building on earlier knowledge.

Within Catholic theological circles over the past few centuries, the relativity of all theological constructs was not generally recognized. Catholic theologians displayed a false certainty concerning the common approach to the systematic theology of sacraments. However, in recent years significant weaknesses in the traditional Catholic theology of sacraments have been pointed out. This awareness results from numerous theological insights and a variety of pastoral experiences, conditioned by a new historical situation. It has stimulated Catholic theologians to work towards a new systematic approach.

The first part of this chapter supplies background for this new direction. A brief sketch of the history of theological reflection on the sacraments covers the period from early Scholastic theologians up through the Second Vatican Council. In particular those aspects are stressed which determined the post-Reformation Catholic understanding up to modern times. Then twentieth century contributions which have proved significant for the recovery of the fullness of the sacramental life of the Church are discussed. The reception of the ideas of modern liturgists and systematic theologians by the Second Vatican Council is also discussed as well as their influence on postconciliar reform of the liturgy.

The second part introduces the relationship between the reflections of the human sciences and of theology on the understanding and practice of the sacraments. In this way attention is drawn to the need for theologians to be sensitive to the contribution which human sciences can make to the theology and effective practice of the sacraments. It also affords the opportunity to point out both valuable contributions and limitations of the human sciences in this sphere of Christian life. For it is certainly true that Christian sacraments cannot be properly understood and practiced unless theological reflection and pastoral implementation bear in mind that the Body of Christ relates to the laws of historical human existence.

In the dialogue between the human sciences and theology, it is imperative that the different methods and goals of each be kept in mind. The object under investigation in both cases is the external practice and Christian interpretation of ritual worship. But the human sciences cannot assume that the interpretation of the meaning, conditions of efficacy, and the efficacy itself of Christian worship is logically irreducible beyond the interpretation of Christian faith. They base their findings on objective evidence and leave open the question of the truth of faith's claim to the transcendent dimension. On the other hand, theology assumes that the interpretation of all aspects of Christian worship is ultimately the responsibility of correct faith. While correct faith, understood as knowledge of faith, admits of degrees regarding the penetration of the mystery of Christian worship, it always tends towards the truth in its fullness.

But even if theological reflection on the claim of faith has the prior claim to a hearing, the neglect of the insights furnished by human sciences leads to a truncated presentation of the meaning and less effective practice of the sacraments. These ritual actions of the Church are understandable to the extent that they are integrated into the mystery of the life of the Church, the paschal mystery of the life, death, and resurrection of Christ. They are neither more nor less than a means of participation in that mystery. Still they cannot be explained or correctly practiced without reference to their historical dimension.

The Church on earth is the Body of Christ insofar as it exists in history. It cannot dispense with the laws which govern the existence and growth of human communities. Hence the sacraments of the Church must be situated within the totality of symbolic actions and celebrations of life in both the so-called profane and the religious spheres. In other words, reflection on the meaning and effective celebration of sacraments must take into account the laws which govern all truly humanizing celebrations of life. Only in this way can the danger be avoided of constructing an esoteric theology of the sacraments and isolating liturgical practice from human life in general and the whole of Christian existence in particular.

Human sciences can contribute a great deal to the clarification of the presuppositions for an effective celebration and to the explanation of the role of sacraments in the personal communication between the saving God and believer. Obviously they cannot do everything. Christian faith itself gives its own interpretation to the chief rites of the Church. But sacraments do not refer only to an appeal of God made to believers. They likewise refer to the horizontal aspect of the history of saving faith which has its origin in the incarnate Lord. Sacramental celebrations make clear that human existence reposes, in its concrete form, on the horizontal level. It is an existence which is mediated in and through history and realized only by historical mediation, also as human existence in faith. Consequently a sacramental theology cannot ignore the data supplied by human sciences, which is based on the analysis of the historical side of sacramental celebrations. Rather, it should be constructed in such a way that the insights provided by the human sciences accompany and support theological reflection at each step of its progress in the understanding of sacraments.

The final section brings together a number of insights which have been discussed or alluded to in the previous two parts. This provides the framework for a new approach to the theology of sacraments which begins by situating them within the history of salvation and the sacramental structure of all created reality. It concludes by explaining how sacraments, as acts of the faith of the Church, are peculiar instances of the way in which God's presence is realized as saving presence within human history. This analysis of the nature and efficacy of sacraments leads to the conclusion that sacraments are not accurately described as means of grace which presuppose the participants to be fully constituted subjects. Rather, the participants are made subjects of God's self-communication through the sacramental celebration itself. From this point of view, sacraments are the shape of God's grace in the form of the expression of the faith of the Church of which Christ in the Spirit is the living source.

Salient Features of Catholic Theology of Sacraments

Origin of Systematic Theology of Sacraments

A sacrament is a sign instituted by Christ to confer the grace which it signifies. This brief description of an essential aspect of the traditional chief rites of the Church derives from the twelfth century attempts to get at the heart of the problem: what constitutes a principal rite of the Church? But the full meaning originally intended by this formula can only be grasped by reading the treatises in which it is found. For example, Hugo of St. Victor (died 1141) uses a similar formulation which is set within his understanding of the history of salvation. This creative theologian, whose theology of sacraments exercised a decisive influence on the high Scholastics, begins with the question: since sacraments are intended for human beings, what is the actual situation of humanity in the history of salvation? Only by answering this, could he make sense out of the role of sacraments in the life of faith.

The early and high Scholastics had great powers of synthesis. They employed them to the best of their ability in the attempt to shed light on the meaning of sacraments in relation to all aspects of the economy of salvation. Instinctively they knew that an adequate grasp of the chief rites of the Church could only be achieved by situating them within the whole of God's activity in history and in relation to the human condition of sinfulness. Above all the sacraments had to be related to the incarnation and life of Jesus Christ, as well as to the Church of which he is head. Since sacraments are signs of grace, these theologians grounded them on Christ, the one mediator of all grace. Since they are activities which take place in the milieu of the Church, theology sought to show how sacraments are linked to the Church.

Sacraments are "efficacious signs of grace." This technical medieval formulation, which draws partially on the teaching of St. Augustine, is one way of expressing the traditional conviction, based on the liturgical experience, that sacramental celebrations are a means of communication in which the Father through Christ in the Spirit bestows and deepens the new life in Christ. But another part of the whole tradition, grounded on the same liturgical experience, teaches that the sacramental deepening of the new life is conditioned by the grateful response of believers made possible by the gift of faith. Consequently, systematic theology undertook the difficult task of explaining how the divine initiative and response of faith come together in the celebration of a sacrament.

The synthesis of sacramental theology resulting from the work of twelfth and thirteenth century scholars is impressive. Despite its limitations it was not equaled during the later Scholastic period nor indeed down to the modern era.

Post-Tridentine Developments

From the high Scholastic period to recent times, Catholic theology possessed a common doctrine of the sacraments. Despite intramural debates a similar approach was maintained, as well as agreement on major issues. In the wake of the sixteenth century Reformation upheaval, an even more unified theology was formulated, which tended to efface even the superficial differences between the various schools of theology. The Reformers criticized many of the traditionally unassailable doctrinal positions relating to sacraments. In this polemical situation the Council of Trent was forced to take a stand on several important issues. These included the number of the principal rites of the Church instituted by Christ and the relation between the seven sacraments and the bestowal of sacramental grace, that is, the special participation of the grace of Christ, the head of the Church, proportioned to the purpose of each sacrament.

This council had no intention of saying everything that could be affirmed about sacraments. Its teaching does not include the fullness of the theology of St. Thomas Aquinas and other first-rank theologians of the high Middle Ages. Still its tentative doctrinal synthesis became the basis for the theological expositions of subsequent Catholic theologians. This is not the place to describe in detail all the features of the post-Reformation Catholic theology of the sacraments. Only the peculiar traits can be mentioned which decisively determined the Catholic understanding up through the beginning of the twentieth century.

This school of theology describes sacraments as objective means of grace and as instrumental causes of grace which the Church has at its disposal. While sacraments are understood to signify and cause grace, the sign function is relegated to a back seat. It serves to distinguish one sacrament from another and to awaken the faith of the recipient to respond appropriately to the particular sacramental grace offered in each sacrament. The connection between Church and sacraments, just as the link between the signifying and causal functions of sacraments, is very weak. The sacraments are not precisely identified as acts of the Church itself but as acts of the minister of Christ's Church which take place in the Church. The role of Christ, his active participation in the celebration of sacraments, is also given scarce attention except in the case of the Eucharist.

It is especially noteworthy that this theology only marginally considered the role of the Holy Spirit in the sacraments, although the Spirit was viewed as the source of sanctification in the life of the Church. This was due to Catholic theology's inability to attribute a personal mission to the Spirit in the economy of salvation which went beyond appropriation. For traditional Catholic theology viewed the sanctifying work of the Trinity as common to all the three persons and attributed it to the Spirit because it was appropriate to the Spirit's name. This lack of pneumatology in the

systematic theology of sacraments had an influence on the infrapersonal concept of the sanctifying grace bestowed through sacraments.
Still other presuppositions more directly supported this point of
view.

Sacramental grace, the grace proper to each sacrament, is
understood to include sanctifying grace. This latter grace, a supernatural elevating grace, is described in neo-scholastic theology as
a supernatural disposition which qualifies human nature for union
with uncreated grace, the indwelling Trinity. Especially after the
Council of Trent neo-scholasticism developed the distinction between created grace (equals supernatural elevating grace) and uncreated grace (equals God communicating self with God's own
nature) in such a way that a certain disjunction was postulated between them. In other words their copresence in the soul of the just
person was not seen as necessary but only factual. The common
view of Catholic theology regarded uncreated grace as more or less
the complement of created grace.

This theology of sanctifying grace is based on a theology of pure
nature which conceives human nature as closed on itself, granted
a natural end. Divine grace intervenes gratuitously as a super-
additum thus conferring a supernatural end. Grace, therefore, remains an exterior complement to nature and is placed in the range
of accident of nature.

This extrinsicism in the doctrine of grace is now severely criticized
by both conservative and progressive Catholic theologians. It is
viewed as a degradation of the concept of grace linked to an understanding of grace which is deprived of historical foundation and
proceeding from infrapersonal categories. Catholic theology now
tends to consider the personal self-communication of the Trinity
in the Spirit as the uncreated grace which is the essential basis for
the whole of the human being's grace-given endowment. From this
point of view, actual grace is simply the self-communication of God
in its dynamic aspect of seeking to evoke the free response of the
human being. It can be called efficacious or merely sufficient insofar as it meets with acceptance or rejection on the part of the free
human being.

This new approach includes the presupposition that created grace
is everywhere as the active orientation of human beings towards
God's self brought about by God's self-communication. Grace
events, which occur at definite points of space and time, are the
historical acceptance of God's own communication of self by which

the personal union between the human being and the divine is realized.

This understanding of grace has important consequences for the theology of the grace event of sacramental celebrations. Sacraments do not appear as isolated instances in which God acts in space and time to confer grace, as in the neo-scholastic construct. Rather sacraments can be said to confer grace insofar as they afford the context in which God's offer of self-communication, as the goal of human existence and the inmost motive force towards this goal, is existentially accepted.

EARLY-TWENTIETH-CENTURY CONTRIBUTIONS OF LITURGISTS

A new approach to sacramental theology took root in the early part of the twentieth century within the field of liturgical studies. Among the contributors to this movement must be mentioned Dom Odo Casel. His theology of mysteries brought to the foreground the central message of Christian tradition: the permanent, active presence of the Risen Lord and his saving acts in the Church, especially in its liturgical celebrations.

According to Casel, the forgotten truth about Christianity is its ontological basis. The exclusive subjective orientations in modern spirituality, which depict Christianity as a reality of the psychological order, are opposed to the traditional outlook which considers Christianity as primarily a reality of the ontological order. What makes Christianity unique among religions is the elevation of the human person's whole being through participation in the mystery of Christ's transition from suffering to glory which is made objectively present under the symbolic expressions of Christian faith. From this participation through faith, there flows the new moral life. The ethical life is, therefore, the new form of life in Christ as it blossoms on the level of concrete historical acts.

Casel's theological synthesis stresses that grace is primarily Christ himself and his whole redemptive work, the kernel of which is his passover from suffering to glory. Grace is not only a power flowing from this mystery of redemption. This grace, accomplished once for all under the conditions of history, remains always accessible to the Church on earth, especially in its liturgy. Through the liturgy believers come into contact with the mystery of redemption, which is objectively present, and continually deepen their participation in the holiness which Christ possesses in fullness. According to Casel this understanding, which is supported by the liturgy's witness, was lost sight of through Scholastic theology's unilateral stress on the grace given to the subject of the sacrament. The ancient Christians, on the contrary, looked first to the objective mystery content of the sacraments.

Casel's teaching did not receive unqualified support from Catholic theologians or the teaching authority of the Roman Catholic Church. Its weaknesses cannot be overlooked. This holds for his speculation about the mode of the presence of Christ's passover in the liturgy. According to him it is a sacramental presence, analogous to Christ's substantial presence in the sacrament of his Body and Blood. Casel's description of the relation of the mystery presence of the redemptive work to the symbolic actions of the liturgy is also open to criticism. Typically he speaks of the presence of the mystery under the veil of symbols. Hence a weak link is established between the liturgical expressions of faith and the mystery presence. Correspondingly the ecclesiological and pneumatological aspects of the liturgy are poorly integrated. Nevertheless, his rediscovery of the fundamental meaning of Christian worship, participation in the paschal mystery, has proved to be a lasting contribution. Casel contributed greatly to the new awareness of the personal aspect of sacramental grace. He also helped to broaden the concept of the sacramental nature of all liturgical acts.

The recovery of the forgotten truth that Christ is actively present in all liturgical activity brought with it a new consciousness of the mystery dimension of every aspect of liturgical celebrations. Not only the essential words and symbolic gestures of the sacraments but also the surrounding liturgical prayers and symbolic actions, scriptural readings, and homily were more clearly seen as complementary ways in which the Lord communicates with his Church and draws it into union with the Father in the Holy Spirit.

The new understanding of the sacramental nature of all liturgical rites and language enclosing the "essential matter and form of the sacraments" was already alive in the rather restricted circle of liturgists and systematic theologians during the Second World War. Their writings, which supported a basic insight of Casel, were uncompromising in the rejection of the interpretation of "ecclesiastical rites" as merely outward dress calculated to prepare the faithful for a sacramental event. The influence of these scholars on Pius XII's encyclical letter, *Mediator Dei*, of November 20, 1947, is well-known. At least since that time it would be incorrect to say that official Catholic theology is insensitive to the profound sacramental nature of the liturgy which provides the context for the brief formulas and symbolic actions which express the heart of the meaning of each sacrament. This encyclical shows how the highest teaching office of the Roman Catholic Church learned from a creative theologian, Casel, that all components of the liturgy of the sacraments are manifestations of the faith of the Church of which Christ in the Spirit is the source. Hence, they all have a sacramental character, that is, manifest and realize a grace event.

In the years following Casel's sudden death, which occurred while he was about to begin the *Exultet* during the paschal vigil of 1948, a number of liturgists and those engaged in the broader study of Christian spirituality initiated a study of the relation between liturgical and other traditional forms of Christian piety. It was commonly recognized that a systematic approach to this subject was needed to give direction to the liturgical renewal which had already begun. This study is still in an embryonic stage. Books on the subject of sacramental spirituality have scarcely touched the surface. However, for our purposes it is sufficient to observe that early in the liturgical movement liturgists recognized, at least implicitly, that the structure of grace events is identical both in the celebration of sacraments and in the daily life of believers. In other words, they were not inclined to describe the sacraments as cheap sources of grace. The witness of the liturgy itself indicates that the same response of faith on the part of the subject of sacramental grace is required to deepen union with God.

Correspondingly, liturgists emphasized the link between daily life and common worship. They described the various forms of common worship as constitutive of the historical Church, correlative and coextensive with its stability and growth. This view was championed by Pius XII in *Mediator Dei*. Both contemporary scholarship and the official teaching of the Church prior to the Second Vatican Council showed concern to establish and foster the relation between the daily preaching of the Gospel, liturgy, and Christian service of love.

However, this pastoral preoccupation had to face two major obstacles. The traditional official theology of sacraments was inadequate to explain the newer insights, and the practice of the sacraments had become marginally relevant in the lives of a great number of baptized Catholics. These problems stimulated systematic theologians to undertake the task of rethinking the meaning of this basic Christian activity.

PRECONCILIAR SYSTEMATIC THEOLOGY

We have already treated the understanding of grace developed by systematic theologians in reaction to the extrinsicism of neo-scholasticism. This new approach, which initially evoked a negative reaction from the Roman magisterium, had already taken hold prior to the Second Vatican Council although its implications for a theology of sacraments had not been worked out. Two other contributions to the renewal of sacramental theology made prior to the completion of the Second Vatican Council must also be mentioned. The first concerns the relation between faith and sacraments, the second the relation between Church and sacraments.

One of the chief merits of the slim volume of Edward Schillebeeckx, *Christ the Sacrament of the Encounter with God*, is its clear and convincing articulation of the basis for a more personalistic approach to the chief rites of the Church.[1] According to him, the response of faith given by the participants of the sacraments is an integral part of the whole liturgical act. He argued that the personal offer of grace by Christ in the sacraments requires a similar response by the believers. In this way he brought to light and effectively dispelled the remnants of the possible misunderstanding of the "automatic efficacy" of sacraments which is often associated in the popular mind with the formula "sacraments confer grace *ex opere operato.*"

By the time of the opening session of the Second Vatican Council on October 11, 1962, Schillebeeckx's personalistic explanation and some of its main implications had received wide acceptance. Karl Rahner, among others, made a notable contribution to this subject. But his name is associated in a special way with a new understanding of the Church's relationship to the sacraments which he worked out in *The Church and the Sacraments.*[2] According to Rahner, the Church should not be conceived as dispenser of the sacraments which, absolutely speaking, could be entrusted to some other institution. Rather the Church "dispenses" sacraments because they are nothing other than acts of the Church by which the Church actualizes itself as agent of Christ for the benefit of individual believers in particular situations of life. In short they are acts which flow from the very nature of the Church.

This conclusion led Rahner to describe the Church as a sacrament: the efficacious sign of God's decisive and abiding turning to the world in Jesus Christ. It further stimulated him to work out a more precise formulation of the mutual relation between the preaching of the Gospel and the sacraments which employ this same word. As a result he describes sacraments as no more or less than the most intensive form of the proclamation of the Word of God directed to individuals in concrete situations of the life of faith.

SECOND VATICAN COUNCIL

Influenced by the gains of modern liturgists and systematic theologians, the Second Vatican Council attempted to integrate many of their contributions into its description of sacraments. The Constitution on the Sacred Liturgy, *Sacrosanctum Concilium*,[3] refers to the relationship between the participants' faith and the fixed forms of expression of faith of sacramental celebrations in such a way as to challenge theologians to think more deeply about the relation between faith and sacraments. Concerning sacraments it states: "They not only presuppose the faith, but through words and things also nourish it, strengthen it and express it. That is why they are called sacraments of faith" (SC 59). The sacramental function of the verbal element of sacraments, alluded to in this pregnant passage, as well as the similar role of word in the whole of the liturgy, is highlighted elsewhere. For example, an analogy is drawn between the Eucharistic "table fellowship and the table of the word of God" (SC 51). The Church is also understood as a sacramental reality: "The sacrament of unity" (SC 26). Thereby the relation of Church to sacraments is placed in a new light. However, further development of the sacramental nature of the Church is left to the Dogmatic Constitution on the Church, *Lumen Gentium*.[4]

Lumen Gentium states that "The Church, in Christ, is like a sacrament, that is a sign and instrument of the intimate union with God and of the unity of the whole human race" (LG 1). In another place it speaks of the Church as "universal sacrament of salvation" (LG 48). Thus it affirms that the Church is not only an abiding sign of what God has already accomplished but minister of Christ in the work of salvation.

This understanding of the Church offers access to a better grasp of the relation between Church and sacraments. It contains the implicit notion that the Church itself makes the sacraments and is made by the sacraments. *Lumen Gentium* seems to be inspired by this thinking when it speaks of the Eucharist under the care of the bishop as a means by which "the Church continually grows and lives" (LG 26). Elsewhere this constitution refers more clearly to the idea that the Church makes the sacraments: "The sacred nature and

organic structure of the priestly community is brought into opera-
tion through the sacraments" (LG 11). This section also indicates
how the various sacraments make the Church.

As a corollary to the notion that the Church makes the
sacraments by the activity of the priestly community and so is renewed by them, *Sacrosanctum Concilium* underscores the importance of the active participation of the cocelebrants, clergy and laity
(SC 11, 27, 48, 50). The main goal of the liturgical renewal is said
to be the "full and active participation of all the people" (SC 14).
But this program can only be realized by the personal communication between the participants. *Sacrosanctum Concilium* recognizes
this and, indeed, employs a way of speaking which is reminiscent
of the language and perspectives of the science of communication.
It emphasizes the need for understandable rites (SC 34, 72) and
linguistic exchange (SC 36, 54). In this way communication is
described as pertaining to the essence of the liturgical celebrations
of the Church.

This communication is understood to go beyond that which is
realized between the believing participants. "For in the liturgy God
speaks to his people, and Christ is still proclaiming his gospel. And
the people reply to God by song and prayer" (SC 33). Here the constitution affirms that the communication between believers through
the expression of the faith of the Church is the means of communication between God/Christ and the community. But how can the
expression of the faith of the Church, witnessing to the revelation
of God in Christ, be construed as the appeal of God in Christ to
the community?

It is not possible to provide a detailed explanation of this problem. But a brief one is called for, since it is relevant to a theology
of sacraments. We can begin by distinguishing between the content of faith, the act of faith, and the witness of faith. The content
of faith—that which is believed—is God revealing self in Christ as
redeemer, or the Christ-event culminating in the death and resurrection of Jesus of Nazareth. The act of faith corresponds to this
ultimately personal and so ungraspable content of faith. Both the
content of faith and the act of faith always remain identical.
However, the interpretation of the content of faith, corresponding
to the act of faith, undergoes changes in conceptual expression in
new cultural and historical situations.

The act of faith obtains the power to find the conceptual expression corresponding to the content of faith in the interpretation

of Scripture. For Scripture is the first and normative witness to the content of faith. However, the act of faith obtains the power to interpret Scripture within the ecclesiastical community, for only to it has the guidance of the Spirit been promised. In the end Word and Spirit provide the security that all believe in the same Lord in whom the apostles believed.

The formulations of the content of faith are necessary so that all may perceive, hear, and respond to that content, God revealing self in Christ. But since the content of faith, the revealing God, is eminently personal, it follows that the liturgy is not primarily concerned with giving instruction about Christian doctrine. For liturgy has to do with worship. Consequently, the constitution teaches that the liturgy should not be concerned with merely giving information but should include the type of activity which affectively moves the participants so that "their minds are raised to God" (SC 33).

The source of the truly communicative activity between God and the community is mentioned early on in *Sacrosanctum Concilium*. It is the active presence of Christ "especially in her liturgical celebrations" (SC 7). He is depicted as the chief speaker and actor of the community who communicates with his members through the expression of the faith of the Church of which he, in the Spirit, is the vital source. As a result the faithful are aroused and made capable of interacting with their Lord and so addressing the Father of all.

This brief description of some of the contributions of the Second Vatican Council toward the formulation of a new theology of the sacraments may serve to indicate its overall approach. The council refrained from formulating dogmatic definitions and sought to grasp the meaning of sacraments from the pastoral point of view. Hence, it encourages reflection which begins from the liturgical rites themselves. We will return to this subject in a later section of this chapter.

POSTCONCILIAR REFORM OF THE LITURGY

Perhaps the most significant impulse for a new theology of sacraments was provided by the liturgical reform of the rites. This reform calls for catechetical instruction anterior to the celebration of the sacraments, encourages some commentary in the liturgy itself, and provides for the expanded use of Scripture and preaching. All of this reflects the pastoral concern which we have mentioned previously: the need to enlighten the faithful about the meaning of the sacraments which is not self-evident. At the same time it becomes a daily reminder to theologians of their responsibility to furnish a new explanation of sacraments which is more in tune with the modern mentality and the witness of the liturgy itself.

The reform of the liturgy also increased the opportunity for a more active participation of both clergy and laity. The implementation of this legislation gives dramatic evidence that sacraments are to be understood as self-realizations of the Church or, more precisely, as communal actions by which a concrete Christian community realizes itself. This new law of liturgical practice is the playing out of the theological premise that the Church realizes itself in sacramental celebrations. Therefore, it offers the best tangible argument for an approach to the theology of sacraments that begins with the worshipping community.

This approach has already provided a corrective to an abstract concept of the real subject of liturgical celebrations. For several hundred years up through the middle of the twentieth century, Catholic theology had taken for granted that in some way the holy members of the universal Church throughout the world actively participated in each official liturgical action. This was explained as resulting from their intention to unite their prayer with the official prayer of the Church. As a consequence it was assumed that their devotion contributed to the measure of the blessings bestowed by God as a response to the liturgical action. This theory, which has yet to be fully set aside in many circles, supplies a basic premise for the conclusion that all Masses, as acts of the Church, are the occasion for the bestowal of God's blessings on the Church and world.

Nowadays it is more clearly understood, at least in professional theological circles, that the devotion of the holy people throughout the world can only be related to the efficacy of liturgical prayer in a very restricted sense. This devotion, through its witness, contributes to the strengthening of the faith of those who actually engage in the liturgy.

It is somewhat ironic that some theologians who readily accept the correction of the traditional theological explanation of the role of the whole Church in the Masses of the world employ an abstract ecclesiological approach in their systematic theology of sacraments. Instances of this are found more frequently in popular writers who rely too much on Karl Rahner's theoretical discussion of principles governing the ecclesiological grounding of sacraments.

Rahner speaks of the Church as *basic sacrament* and of sacraments as instances of the Church realizing itself as the new people of God that lives in Christ and has the task of extending Christ's saving work in the world. But it is clearly not his intention to distinguish between the universal Church and local communities in such a way that the universal Church is understood as a distinct entity. His contribution to the rejection of the idea that the devotion of the universal Church directly measures the blessings derived from the official prayer of the Church is sufficient to show how concretely he thinks.

It can be safely said that there is no universal Church which has a place against and over the local communities and which realizes itself in the activity of the local communities. The Church exists historically and visibly where a community of faithful lives an ordered life according to the Gospel and ecclesiastical tradition. These communities, living in communion with one another, are truly churches and are the basic sacrament from which the sacramental celebrations derive. The experience which results from the active participation of all in the liturgy of the local community can do much to make the participants aware that they are the basic sacrament from which sacraments derive. However, this happens to the extent that the local community is able to identify the ultimate source of this experience: Christ, the head of the Church.

The Christological turn of the liturgical theology of the Second Vatican Council offers a helpful insight in this regard. The teaching about the active presence of Christ in all activities of the Church (SC 7) should make Catholics aware that the Church can only be called sacrament in a very restricted sense. The term itself points to the fact that the Church has the mission from Christ to unfold his saving work in the world as his servant.

The Church is a kind of sacrament where it manifests that Christ's redemptive work, accomplished in his life, death, and resurrection, continues to be effective in this world. Consequently, it can be called a sacrament insofar as the members' fidelity to the Gospel demonstrates them to be a redeemed people of God and insofar as they extend Christ's promise of salvation to one another and to those called to join their ranks. Indeed, the holiness of the community and its missionary character are inseparable. The community that lives in union with Christ necessarily reaches out as minister of Christ to draw all those for whom Christ died into its midst.

Human Sciences and the Sacraments

The various Christian theological traditions agree in principle that communal worship is an essential ingredient of the life of faith. But its precise role has been explained in different ways. No one doubts that it can contribute to a deepening of the life of faith. Still in post-Reformation neo-scholasticism, as well as in classical Reformation theology, this aspect is stressed insofar as specific forms of Christian worship can be said to contain sacraments instituted by Christ to confer the grace they signify. Otherwise, the accent falls on the human act of worship of God. Undoubtedly, this point of view is influenced, consciously or unconsciously, by a specific theological understanding of the goal of creation of human beings.

Characteristically, post-Reformation theology argued that the goal of creation must correspond to something worthy of God's self. Since this can only be God, the conclusion was drawn that the ultimate goal of creation is the extrinsic glory of God. The word extrinsic is used to indicate that the glory given to God does not touch God intrinsically. The logical consequence of this theory makes the ultimate goal of Christian worship the extrinsic praise offered to God on account of God's perfection. In short it is the affirmation of the right ordering of creator and creature. The fact that creatures open themselves to receive God's blessings through explicit witness to their dependence represents a proximate goal of creation and worship.

There is, however, an older tradition which considers worship as primarily ordered to the fulfillment of creatures. It is related to the idea that God created the world to share divine goodness. From this perspective prayer is a means of cooperation with God's ultimate reason for creation of human beings, namely, to share God's goodness. A classical formulation of this view is found in St. Irenaeus of Lyons. He explains that God instituted sacrifices for human needs. Others, such as St. Thomas Aquinas, teach that we pray not because God needs our prayers but because we need to pray in order to be open to the reception of God's grace.

This old view has been resurrected in modern times. For example, the Sunday Mass obligation is no longer grounded on the natural law obligation of the creature to give due honor to God. It is much more firmly based on the law of the Gospel: the obligation of supporting one's own life of faith through participation in the community of faith to whom the promise of the Spirit has been given. Consequently, the liturgy is not given the basic structure of a monologue. Rather, it is viewed as involving a dialogue between God and the community, in which the accent falls on what is ultimately signified by the liturgical expression of the faith of the Church, God's sanctifying activity. *Sacrosanctum Concilium* almost always stresses this orientation. For example, it states: "From the liturgy . . . grace is poured forth . . . and the sanctification of people and the glorification of God . . . are achieved with maximum effectiveness" (SC 10). Consequently, the need for active participation so that believers will be open to engage in this dialogue and to cooperate in the goal of redemption, which corresponds to the goal of creation, becomes a major concern of this constitution.

The recovery of the awareness of the dialogue structure of Christian worship has stimulated the interest of liturgists and theologians in the contributions which human sciences might make to a better understanding of the nature of sacraments and the presuppositions for effective worship. For it is also understood that this dialogue takes place in history and so falls under the laws of human communication. Some of the results of the interdisciplinary cooperation between human sciences and sacramental theology are discussed below.

Anthropological-Christological Basis of Sacramental Rites

Sacramental rites employ doxological and rhetorical language enriched by images drawn from a variety of spheres of human life. Together with symbolic actions, the "word" signifies a concrete human and social situation, for example, the decision of partners to enter married life. At the same time the word announces that God's saving presence is to be found in this situation and tells how the recipient is to respond. In short, sacramental rites refer to the more fundamental sacramental meaning of human situations.

Modern anthropology sheds light on how this type of activity corresponds to the actual nature of human beings. It draws on phenomenology's description of the human being as a whole, how it appears to the senses in its moods and presuppositions. This science shows that the human person is *spirit in body*, a being that develops through contact with the surrounding environment and other persons.

Beginning with this view of the human being, anthropology describes the human body as the most original symbol of the individual. However, while the body is the most original appearance and source of self-knowledge, it is not static. It grows, waxes, wanes, and succumbs. In this process particular junctures of the biological life become sources of new self-understanding. There are situations, such as puberty and aging, which cannot be manipulated but only accepted as inevitable stages. They can be called boundary situations because, despite the freedom which a human being experiences to make changes and to manipulate things and people, they reveal the weakness of a person to overtake and master oneself. In short, they manifest the finitude of the human being and so raise the question of the meaning of life. There are also similar situations which occur in the social life. The call to make a decision about the course of one's adult life or to come to the aid of other human beings who make unconditional demands in their absolute need cannot be manipulated.

These situations are never experienced in a vacuum. For the society in which we live provides us with a timely word which interprets these situations and so excludes or includes different possibilities of meaning and choice. The word illumines the human situation and so provides the key to the response we must make in order to give meaning and direction to our lives.

By relating this data to sacramental celebrations, theologians are able to show that the unity of word and symbolic gesture in the sacraments has a solid anthropological basis. For the seven sacraments symbolize and interpret the meaning of important situations in the lives of believers which are ambivalent in themselves. However, the theologian cannot remain content with this anthropological explanation of the sacraments. For the whole Christian tradition, in one way or another, traces the practice of sacraments back to Jesus Christ. Since the sixteenth century this is usually done by searching for an implicit or explicit word of institution by the historical Jesus. For example, Jesus is said to have insinuated his will to institute the sacrament of the sick when he cured the sick. In recent times Catholic theology recognizes that this approach is too superficial. Now the practice of the seven sacraments is founded on the deeper meaning of the incarnation itself and the daily preaching and symbolic actions of Jesus' public life.[5]

In the incarnation the Word of God entered the human situation by taking flesh from the Virgin. Here it is revealed that the presence of the Divine Son is to be found in its most radical form in the man Jesus of Nazareth. Through personal contact with him, one meets the Son of God himself. Moreover, in his public ministry Jesus announces to his audiences that they must seek God in their ordinary circumstances of daily life and respond in accord with Jesus' Gospel. For example, Jesus gives instruction as to how one is to respond when another offends one many times: forgive always.

When we consider sacramental celebrations from this viewpoint, it is evident that they are paradigms for the whole range of possible instances of relating the Word of God to concrete situations of life. The whole life of Christ furnishes the Church with the reason why it can and indeed must announce a timely word of Christ in common social situations in the life of the Church, if it is to remain faithful to the revelation and example of its head, Jesus Christ.

Symbolic Competence

The postconciliar legislation, aimed at renewal of the liturgy, directs those responsible for religious formation to provide catechetical instruction both anterior to and in the sacramental celebrations. This presumes that the meaning of the sacraments is not self-evident to many Catholics. In one way or another the first two chapters of this book touched on this problem by raising the issue of *symbolic competence*, the capacity of a Christian to link traditional liturgical symbols and interpretative word with one's adult personal symbols. They demonstrate that a catechesis of the sacraments must take account of the modern condition of human existence and its influence on the life of faith, as well as the modern contexts in which participants can be expected to respond to sacramental celebrations in a religious way.

Liturgists and theologians can gain valuable information from these thematic human sciences of psychology and sociology, which enable them to carry out their critical function regarding the new sacramental rites and their style of celebration. Phenomenology's contribution must also be mentioned. By studying the human being as a whole, in its moods and presuppositions, this science shows that the experience of the holy belongs to situations in which the question of ultimate meaning is raised. So the distinction between the sacred and profane is placed at the level of understanding. In other words, the profane is always potentially holy if its deepest meaning is penetrated.

The data of phenomenology provides a clue as to how catechesis of the sacraments should begin. A phenomenological introduction to the catechesis of the sacraments is becoming more popular today. It begins with the invitation to the audience to recall their experience of the depth of meaning in ordinary daily happenings.

Many modern songs have their appeal because they likewise lead the hearers to discover a world of meaning in very ordinary occurrences. Here we can cite as an example the words of the popular ballad: "When I wake up in the morning, she says 'Hi,' . . . If that isn't loving me, God didn't make little green apples. . . ." This approach can take the form of a narrative of one's own discovery of meaning in routine living and subsequently in sacramental celebrations. In this way it is possible to show that anything can be a symbol of something transcendent and even of the Transcendent itself. A wide experiential basis can thus be obtained through inner perception of the depth dimension of all reality. This furnishes an important preparation for the liturgy of the sacraments, for the proper intention of sacraments is to serve as manifestations of the divine saving presence.

Promoting Symbolic Competence through the Liturgy

In the second chapter of this book, we have been informed that an effective liturgy invites awareness and celebration of personal symbols and their connection with the biblical and traditional symbols expressed in the liturgy. The liturgist can only agree with these excellent observations and gains valuable insights into the laws which govern effective communitarian activity. However, the science of liturgy has a special orientation which differs from that of the psychologist. First of all, the liturgist is not merely concerned with a style of celebration which promotes the communitarian aspect and enables the participants to somehow connect what is being done with their personal lives. Even less is the liturgist preoccupied with developing forms of liturgy which are so adapted to modern Catholics that they merely convey, and enable the participants to share in, the celebration of some important human values. The problem for the liturgist corresponds to the formal object of the science of liturgy: *the Church, insofar as it accepts the saving work of God in Jesus Christ and prayerfully responds.* So liturgists pose this basic question for themselves: what form of liturgy enables the faithful to participate in the event of God working among his people?

Obviously this question should be approached by asking who is the person being formed through the liturgy and under what conditions is this realized. The anthropological sciences shed a good deal of light on this question, as we have seen in the two previous chapters. But one also must ask about the Church itself. What is this Church that is being built up by the sacraments? What are the possibilities of the liturgical activity of the Church? To know the Church means, in the first place, to know what it can do, and to know this, one must be acquainted with what it has done in the past. So it is evident that the history of the liturgy is important for determining what liturgy is qualified to build up the Church.

From the study of the liturgy of the past, we can recognize what laws of human conduct within the Church enabled previous generations to experience God's saving presence in the liturgy and to name God in a response of praise and thanksgiving. The liturgist is also led back to the Old and New Testaments, the history which records the initial and normative encounters with the God of revelation. There is a great amount of information to be obtained from Scripture about God's names, actions, and way of speaking and about the conditions for answering God. Concrete laws are reflected without which there can exist no nearness of the living God in the public forum. One can cite, as an example, the form of address of God to the people through the prophet: Thus says the Lord God. This corresponds to the letter the Council of Jerusalem sent to Antioch: "It is the decision of the Holy Spirit, and ours too, not to lay on you any burden beyond that which is strictly necessary" (Acts 15:28). The form of expression for the experience of the absence of God, which, nevertheless, petitions God's help (Pss 10; 13; 102 and others), is, perhaps, particularly relevant to a liturgy in the midst of a society which is suspicious of any reference to transcendence and especially to the Transcendent itself. Both the Old and New Testaments provide material and norms for examining the quality and potential of the renewed liturgy and for promoting the experience of God speaking and acting in the midst of the liturgical assembly.

APPRECIATIVE CONSCIOUSNESS

In the first chapter of this book, it was argued that the moods and motivations of people in our culture are those which underlie the drive toward rational attainment of goals via the individual achievements of the culture's members, using persons and things as means. This led to the conclusion that an alternative disposition is needed if sacramental experience is to occur: a disposition which orientates us toward the mysterious dimensions of life. This disposition is described as appreciative consciousness, experiencing something or someone in itself.

The liturgist, as such, is not qualified to judge whether this description of the moods and motivations of persons in our industrial society is accurate. But liturgists must certainly agree that the concept of appreciative consciousness is a necessary condition for the ideal form of participation in the celebration of the sacraments. Beyond that, liturgists, exercising their critical function, actually measure the quality of the Christian liturgy by its contribution to the development of appreciative consciousness. For the model of good liturgy is the primary symbol of faith, the Cross of Christ.

This symbol protests against the subordination of the human person to any worldly power or material thing. At the same time it guarantees the meaning of every activity aimed at the removal of suffering which contributes to the dehumanization of people. Since Christian worship preaches the liberation of all humanity through the Cross of Christ, it should contribute to the disclosure of those common conditions in specific cultures which prevent human growth, that is, the development of centered selves, who are freed to affirm their own worth and contribute to the growth of those around them.

It has been claimed, and to a large extent confirmed, that in the modern industrial world a vast number of people experience a form of slavery in the world of work. The identification of self with one's work results in the loss of one's true identity, one's value as a person. To the extent that this situation obtains, liturgy should make known the need to liberate oneself from the suffering and servitude produced by the pressure of achievement. At the same time it should be so conducted that the participants have the opportunity to play out their resolves to live a life worthy of a human being in the field of daily work. In this way Christians could be helped to develop a freeing existence which enables them to make sense of the Gospel message about their destiny to share with others in the blessings of the fulfilled kingdom of God.

This style of liturgy can help to generate the experience of one's absolute worth and that of the other participants. It fosters the display of love among the participants which enables each to recognize self as an individual who is loved by God. But, of course, the liturgy cannot be expected to shoulder the whole responsibility for this appreciative consciousness. Some preparation is needed which begins with contemplation in daily life of the mystery of the human being.

Phenomenology of Religious Worship

Religious worship falls within the scope of the more general phenomenon known as celebration. Humanizing celebrations are communal activities in which a group of like-minded people gather to clarify and fulfill their human existence. In such celebrations ordinary forms of expression of daily life are no longer directed to the opportunities and demands of routine living. Rather they are stylized so as to express enduring realities and values hidden in day-to-day activity. They are needed to bring these values to the surface and to foster them. The fruit of such gatherings is decisions about one's conduct in daily life.

Corresponding to the purpose of celebrations in general, religious worship responds to the need of people to formulate a collective experience of overcoming negativity and to affirm that human existence has meaning despite the constant experience of nonmeaning. Accordingly, three major functions of religious worship can be differentiated: orientation, expression, and affirmation. Communal worship communicates instruction about meaningful, goal-directed activity. It is a medium in which the participants can express their relationship to the divine. Finally, it affirms them in their quest for renewal.

Christian worship displays these three functions in a way proper to it. It is the public communication of the Christian experience of salvation in the medium of the scriptural and ecclesiastical tradition. Christian liturgy recalls the past history of God's saving activity and the kinds of responses in concrete situations of life which made a difference in the lives of individuals and whole communities. But to make a difference in the modern Church, the liturgy must show how this history can provide answers to modern problems which Christians face in daily living. Here the homily has a special role. But also the liturgical rites should reflect an image of God which corresponds to a loving Father who takes his people seriously and an image of Christians as responsible, free people who have their gifts to share with one another.

However, liturgy is not intended to merely provide information about meaningful, goal-directed existence. It aims to be a source of affirmation of God's love for the participants. A good liturgy not only preaches that God loves the sinner but enables the faithful to experience this love which overcomes anxiety and guilt and issues in unshakeable confidence in the faithful God. Consequently, it provides the medium in which believers are able to express their lives and their deepest hopes and aspirations and experience their liberation from forces which tend to dehumanize them.

The uniqueness of religious worship, from a phenomenological point of view, lies in its intention to bring to the surface of the lives of participants not simply one or other human values but contact with the ground of all reality, God.

A religious community gathers together in the hope that its worship will become the medium of the advent of God. The ritual action is a concrete form of confession that the community does not possess all truth. It is a practice of hope that the community can learn anew, from the advent of the divine Truth itself, the deepest meaning of human existence. Moreover, since religious worship announces the advent of the divine, which renews the lives of the participants, it also says something about human works. It teaches that the faithful should not base their expectations on their own powers but on the One who alone can give meaning to all responsible human effort. In this way effective worship wards off discouragement based on human failure and the pressure of achievement and opens up new possibilities for daily life.

The categories of efficacy, truth, and human dignity, derived from authentic religious worship, are relevant to a theology of the sacraments. Sacraments, which are a form of worship, announce God's coming; the participants can only take the posture of openness to this advent. The efficacy of the sacraments relates to the renewal of the whole person, which results from the spiritual penetration and acceptance of the mystery of the divine activity at work in the human expression of faith. Through this engagement the faithful are equipped to live a fully human, freeing existence in the world.

Efficacy of Communicative Actions of Social Groups

Social groups must come together regularly to preserve their identity. Their cohesion is realized by fixed communal actions, which recall the original activity of the persons who founded the organization and which reflect the common day-to-day life of the members. In these gatherings the repetition of the charter which defines the goals and hopes of the group and the symbolic actions which express the social unity effect a kind of new beginning. A new joining together of the members takes place, and they become vitally conscious of their opportunities and tasks of a practical kind. One can think of the gathering of a political party before an election or the annual meeting of a fraternal organization.

All religious communities have an analogous set of images of common life which are displayed in worship. In particular, Christian liturgy is a means by which the Christian community is newly constituted as the Body of Christ. This communal activity recalls the original activity of Christ and his disciples which constituted the Church and the meaning of membership in the Church. Thereby it generates a new beginning of the community. But, as with all social groups, this effect is conditioned by the active participation of the believers who express the faith they live by in daily life. For, as communicative action of a concrete community, the liturgy brings to the surface the gifts which are already given with the gift of faith: the saving presence of God and personal union with Christ in the Church through participation in the Holy Spirit. But this activity is needed because the members of the Church exist in history and must continually celebrate their common faith lest they lose their identity as the Body of Christ.

Liturgy as Event of Divine-Human Communication

The *Constitution on the Sacred Liturgy* qualifies Christian worship as a communicative activity. It encourages the application of a modern theoretical approach to the description of how an event of communication takes place through speech and symbolic action in a social group. However, the application of a modern theory of communication must respect the peculiar nature of Christian worship: the self-communication of God through human communication. This means that a description of the event of communication of liturgy must take into account both the fact of God's saving activity and the medium of human communication.

Beginning with the liturgical act itself, one recognizes that the doxological and rhetorical language and symbolic actions allow the participants to express their own special needs and particular religious experiences. In this way the liturgy enables the individual to take a stand and to identify oneself within the group. At the same time, however, the liturgy is the expression of the faith of the whole Church. The participants, who share in this faith, are able to express together a common or similar response. In fact, what each one brings of personal faith to the assembly is helped by the common expression of faith to transcend one's limited, personal appropriation of the life of faith. The individuals are able to respond more fully by participating in the experience of the faith of the

Church expressed in the rite and by sharing in the experience of the faith expressed by the other participants.

In this way the participants come to recognize existentially that the liturgy, which expresses praise and thanksgiving for what God has done and is doing in the lives of believers, is the means by which God's self-communication takes place. They are, therefore, led to the conclusion that the fixed expression of the faith of the Church in the liturgical rites, as well as the personal faith expressed by the assembly, are supported by Christ himself as the decisive speaker of God's Word and the high priest of the community's act of worship. Christ is recognized as the unique mediator between God and humanity (1 Tim 2:5; Heb 8:6), who acts through the expression of the faith of the Church of which he, in the Spirit, is the living source.

Summary

Modern anthropology's analysis of the relation of word to the human situation helps to shed light on Jesus' preaching that God is to be found in the human situation and indicates how one is to respond. Taken together, the data contributes to the understanding that sacraments are paradigms for the whole range of possible instances of relating the Word of God to concrete situations of life. It supports the idea that all reality has a sacramental dimension.

The observations on the roles of symbolic competence and appreciative consciousness in the preparation for the liturgy and ways of promoting them through the liturgy speak to the pastoral question concerning the presuppositions which enable a more fruitful participation in the sacraments.

The description of the functions of religious worship provides criteria for the quality of sacramental celebrations which can be expected to elicit a true response of faith and determine their specific efficacy.

The analysis of the efficacy of communicative actions of social groups indicates that it consists in a new beginning conditioned by bringing to the surface the values which already exist in day-to-day living. Applied to Christian sacraments, this means that they are intended to evoke an intensive form of living out the gifts which are already given with the gift of faith.

The remarks on liturgy as events of divine-human communication draw out consequences from the fact that the means is human communication. As such, and corresponding to communicative activity of social groups, it enables the individual to take a stand and identify oneself within the group. Hence, the liturgy appears to have the goal of making the participants subjects of God's self-communication—not passive objects of the bestowal of grace.

Towards a New Theology of the Sacraments

We have outlined some of the significant gains in the theology of sacraments made by scholars who struggle to integrate this activity of the Church into the whole of the economy of salvation. Also, we have mentioned the pastoral orientation of liturgical studies and systematic theology. These fields of research have recognized their responsibilities to respond to the need for an explanation of the sacraments which makes sense to the average Catholic and for a practice of the sacraments which really makes a difference. The third part of this chapter, as the first, begins with the question: what is a sacrament? The various modern insights into the nature and function of sacraments provide the grounds for the beginning of a new synthetic response. When they are brought together, what understanding of sacrament emerges?

This section begins with a description of the place of sacraments within the history of salvation, stretching from creation to the second coming of Jesus Christ. Into this picture is inserted the old Church view of the sacramental structure of all created reality and its relation to the history of salvation. The relevance of this viewpoint for the modern Church is mentioned, as well as its implications for the dogmatic teaching about the seven sacraments. The classical problem about the mode of mediation of the grace of Christ through the sacraments is approached from an ecclesiological perspective, which begins with the analysis of sacramental rites as acts of the believing community. From this consideration several important consequences follow. First, God's self-communication is realized historically through human communication, especially in the liturgy. Second, the sacraments, as expressions of the faith of the Church, are paradigms of the way in which God communicates self to humanity in history. Third, the subjects of the sacraments are the gathered community and the individual in whose favor the sacrament is celebrated. Fourth, all subjects of the sacraments share in the measure of participation in the faith of the Church expressed in the rites. Fifth, sacraments announce the offer of grace and simultaneously enable the individual to transcend one's personal faith commitment so as to accept the offer with thanksgiving. Sixth, from this analysis an important corollary follows: sacraments are not a means of grace vis-á-vis the adult subject in whose favor they are celebrated; rather, they mediate the dispositions by which the individual adult is made fully the subject of the sacramental celebration.

A theology of the sacraments cannot overlook the task of integrating the two poles of the grace event of the sacramental celebrations, the divine action and the human response. By their very nature sacraments are aimed at eliciting a response of faith in the individual in whose favor they are celebrated. As shown below, sacraments do not merely presuppose the proper disposition of an adult participant but mediate it. Hence, the priority of the divine initiative is manifested precisely through the celebration as an act of faith of which God through Christ in the Spirit is the source.

The following discussion of sacramental efficacy takes as its model adult participation. The special case of infant baptism, however, is not incompatible with the theological outlook expressed. In both the case of adult and infant baptism, the priority of the divine initiative is expressed by the decision of the community to baptize the person. This priority is manifested by the adult who presents oneself in faith for baptism. In the case of the infant, it is manifested by those who are inspired by the Spirit to present the infant and who speak in his or her name.

At infant baptism those who sponsor the infant, as well as the whole community, receive the support of the Spirit to fulfill their responsibility for nurturing the infant's growth in Christ. Therefore, the infant is placed in a context which is conducive to his or her spiritual development. However, the rite also announces that God offers the grace of regeneration which cannot be resisted by a personal decision of the infant. In other words, the infant is placed in a new way in the sphere of the Spirit.

According to St. Augustine, the infant simply becomes believer through baptism. The initial disposition to respond personally to God's offer of grace is bestowed. The expansion of the grace of baptism occurs as the subject, baptized in infancy, begins to respond personally to the Gospel. The newer approach to the theology of grace views it as given always and everywhere. It is the active orientation of all human beings towards God's self, grounded on God's self-communication. Baptism of infants is, therefore, a symbolic expression of the personal binding of God to the infant, which goes beyond the fundamental orientation to the divine, resulting from

God's self-communication given gratuitously with human existence. It is, therefore, a clear and irrevocable manifestation of God's choice in favor of the infant as believer.

SACRAMENTS AND SALVATION HISTORY

Where do sacraments fit into salvation history? A response to this question should begin with the objective fact that sacraments are liturgical celebrations of the life of the Church. Consequently, they can only be understood from the essence of the Church. So the more basic question arises: where does the Church fit into salvation history?

Salvation history, God's action in history drawing human beings towards intimate personal communion with God's self, cannot be confined to a period in which a special history of salvation stands out. The special history of salvation, according to the Hebrew Scriptures, began with the covenant between God and Abraham. From the New Testament point of view, it extends to the new covenant in Jesus Christ and beyond that to the sending of the Spirit to the Church. It will be completed when the Risen Lord comes from the future to fulfill both world history and salvation history.

Where does the Church fit into the whole of salvation history? We call history the realized life events of human beings. Events take place in space and time. They have a beginning, a middle, and an end. Consequently, as realized life events they are not simply present. But whether they are life events of individuals or social groups, they are not merely past, for they form the present. Human beings do not continually start from zero point; they exist in a world that is historically formed. Life events, therefore, cannot be considered merely in themselves as discrete events with no bearing on the future.

There is also another reason why life events cannot be considered merely in themselves. The creator is personally present and working in all events of human life. God, active in all common life events, has bound self to history and so bestows meaning on those events. From this it follows that earlier acts of God in history are determinative of later acts. Where one experiences God's special revelation in common life events, turning them into saving events, the historical consciousness recognizes that the concrete divine intervention determines the present human situation. Moreover, God's fidelity, a constant biblical theme, decides the direction of later historical divine interventions in favor of creatures.

This point of view is clearly expressed in the Pauline and

Deuteropauline elaboration of the concept *mysterion.* According to the Apostle Paul, the mystery of God is the plan of God, hidden in God from all eternity. It includes creation of the world, redemption of sinful humanity, and the final fulfillment of all things in Christ. This divine plan is progressively revealed and effected in historical events which continually bring newness from God. Revealed and realized in creation, it showed itself after the fall of human beings in historical events which manifested God's fidelity to humanity in spite of sin. The covenant which God made with Israel pointed to the decisive revelation and realization of the mystery of God which happened in the incarnation, life, death, and resurrection of Jesus Christ. From this point of history onward, all manifestations and realizations of the divine plan are grounded on the Christ event. Thus the communication of the Spirit of God at the first Pentecost is interpreted as the direct consequence of the Christ event. According to the New Testament, the Spirit is sent by the Risen Lord from the Father to establish, maintain, and give increase to the new people of God until the second coming of the Risen Lord.

In the New Testament perspective the one divine plan includes creation, redemption, and eschatological fulfillment. While the theme of redemption is stressed, the New Testament does not overlook the decisive thing: the renewal of all creation, grounded on the historical event of the Cross. Since God, creator and redeemer, is one and the same, all creation and history lies under the unique plan of God. Hence, God's way of acting must be grasped in its unity.

This unity of God's activity is implied in the New Testament teaching that the historical events of redemption and sanctification of humanity take place through creation which has become deformed by sin. Redemption consists in God's acceptance of the flesh of sinners through his Word (Rom 8:3). The Father wills salvation to be grounded through the Word incarnated in the flesh, not as it existed originally in creation but in its historical sinful state. In this way the Word, always present to the world, obtains a new presence. Jesus Christ is the mystery of salvation—the sacrament of salvation—in person. Salvation happens through participation in the mystery of God, which is revealed and realized by and in Jesus Christ in the event of the Cross.

The Cross event is the ultimate historical expression of the self-emptying of the Son who assumed the flesh of sin. The mystery of salvation, realized through the self-emptying and obedience to the Cross, continues to be realized in the world in the power of the Spirit. The sending of the Spirit, from the Father by the Risen Lord, follows the historical event of the Cross as something belonging to that event. In the gift of the Spirit, who forms the Church of Jesus Christ, the many are drawn into the unity of the Trinity and share in the divine life in the way proper to creatures.

This presence of the Spirit in the Church, as Spirit of Jesus Christ, is the proper source of its knowledge and power. The Spirit always was and is present to the world as Spirit of God. But with Pentecost the Spirit obtains a new form of presence in the Church and in the world. The Spirit who animates the Church is the Spirit sent by the Risen Lord. So the Spirit is newly present from this event and in a way historically stamped by it. This Spirit makes the Church to be the presence of the salvation effected by the Christ event and, therefore, the sacrament of salvation.

Since the Church has received the Spirit as pledge (Eph 1:13), through its activity believers experience salvation as already received and yet unfulfilled. Through the Church's word and symbolic actions, even though subject to human frailty, the Father communicates the Spirit to believers through his only Son who redeemed humanity "in the likeness of sinful flesh" (Rom 8:3).

According to the Pauline writings, the Church on earth has a special role to play in the divine plan. It comes into being through Jesus Christ. As Body of Christ, it is the mystery of God revealed and become effective through the Christ event. In its own proper way the Church is the mystery of God. As such, with Christ and in dependence on him, it undertakes the work of further realizing and revealing the mystery of God: "Now, therefore, through the church, God's manifold wisdom is made known . . . in accord with his age-old purpose, carried in Christ Jesus our Lord" (Eph 3:10-11).

Since the Church is the mystery of God, its sacramental celebrations can only be understood from this one mystery. The mystery of salvation is effected in and through the historical event of the Cross. This is the decisive realization of the plan of redemption. Consequently, this mystery recalled in the liturgical celebrations of the Church, is newly presented, applied, and lived by believers now. Moreover, since this mystery includes the gift of the Spirit, the liturgy of the Church, which represents it, mediates the communication of the Trinitarian life.

On the other hand, the liturgical celebrations of the Church employ elements of creation deformed by sin, just as the Father sent his Son into flesh deformed by sin and so realized redemption. Through the word and symbolic action of the liturgy, which draw on word and symbolic actions used in daily life, communication takes place between God and believers. This mediates new being or growth in the new life already realized. The various forms of communication of sacraments correspond to the way in which God communicates with humanity through history. Certainly sacraments have a special place in the economy of salvation. Still, this should not lead to exaggerated notions of the exceptional character of sacraments in comparison with the normal means of communication of the life of faith in daily life. Sacraments should not be explained as simply extraordinary and purely supernatural actions.

Sacraments are special moments in the history of salvation, grounded on the Christ event. Hence, they reveal and realize different ways in which Christians are integrated into the mystery of Christ in different situations of the history of the individual and community. Baptism, by which a candidate is incorporated into the paschal mystery, to use a phrase of *Sacrosanctum Concilium* (5.2), represents participation in the death and resurrection of Christ (Rom 6:4-5). The community as a whole is continually integrated into this salvation through the rite which originated from the Last Supper and which announces Christ's self-offering on behalf of the many (1 Cor 10:16-17; 11:23-26).

The different sacraments are graceful supporters of Christians on their journey toward the kingdom of God. They are related to fundamental situations of the lives of individuals (baptism, confirmation, reconciliation of sinners, anointing of the sick), of individuals together (marriage), of individuals in relation to the service of the community (orders), and of the whole community as such (Eucharist). They are intended to sanctify typically basic situations of the daily life of the Christian in the individual and social spheres (SC 6). They are geared to awaken the awareness that each one shares with the others in the pilgrimage of the whole people of God, that together they are underway towards the completion which comes from God alone (SC 8). Through participation in the sacraments, each one is made conscious of moving from one stage of human life to the next within and supported by the whole community of faith (LG 9, 48). In short, sacramental celebrations play out the promised fulfillment and anticipate it here and now (LG 35).

In the Patristic period the two movements within the history of salvation, the descent of the divine and the ascent of human beings to the divine, are dramatically expressed in terms of a mystery play: "God became man in order that human beings might become divine." This understanding of the divine economy of salvation determines the Patristic theology of worship. Christ and his saving work are understood to be really present in mystery in Christian liturgy as source and guide of the ascent of the faithful to God. The participants of the liturgy, which this theology reflects, experience their personal way to God as a participation in the way of the whole people of God: salvation history, which began with creation, is definitively realized in Jesus Christ and will be fulfilled at his second coming.

In this perspective the Eucharist is the summit of all liturgical celebrations. The Church Fathers understood that all forms of Christian worship have a meaning in themselves. They were not considered as simply a means to an end, that is, a place where Christians gain spiritual nourishment for the work of faith in the world. For it was clearly seen that in the liturgy the holy people of God are concretely manifested and realized, a real anticipation of the final gathering of all in Christ. Consequently, all other activity of the Church was seen as ordered to the liturgy, deriving its orientation, inspiration, and spiritual power from that source. But the various forms of liturgy were judged to find their fulfillment in the Eucharist. Under the conditions of history, that to which all liturgy refers, the unity of the people of God in Christ, is manifested and realized in the most profound way in the Eucharist. Here the community gathers around Christ in the Spirit to share in the anticipated messianic banquet to the glory of the Father.

Sacramental Nature of the Cosmos

Within the liturgical rites of the various sacraments, a hierarchy of values was recognized by Patristic writers. The liturgical rites surrounding the Eucharistic Prayer and communion of the Body and Blood of Christ, or the baptismal bath and Trinitarian formula, were placed at a lower level. But they were never considered to be "merely ecclesiastical rites" without deeper sacramental meaning. On the contrary, they were considered to originate from the faith of the Church. Therefore, they played a role of mediation in the saving work of Christ in the Spirit who inspires their use.

This outlook corresponds to the more general comprehensive view of all created reality and its relation to the history of salvation which prevailed throughout the Patristic and early Middle Ages. In this world view salvation history begins with creation. The Father creates all things through the Word, his Son. Therefore, all creation bears the mark of God's love for humanity, the crown of creation. Even to the lowest level of materiality, creation manifests God's saving presence. To be sure, the chief liturgical rites of the Church were valued as particular concentrations of the sacramental nature of all creation. They were interpreted as the highest manifestations of God's presence in the whole of the cosmos. They were valued as providing a correct understanding of the manifold signs in the world which are manifestations of God's love. In addition the sacraments were acknowledged as the most intense forms of God's self-giving after the incarnation.

The systematic theologians of the twelfth and thirteenth centuries have the same basic outlook. They teach that the Word, who created the world, came in the flesh and established the sacraments to draw humanity into union with himself. At the same time they affirm that created reality, used in the sacraments, attains its full meaning. It does not merely manifest the mystery of God's love but is employed by God to communicate self to believers in the special way signified by each sacrament. Hence, they describe the sacraments as a means of a holy exchange, a *sacrum commercium.*

In the West a profound change took place in the understanding of the real world, which had its roots in the late Middle Ages and blossomed in the seventeenth and eighteenth centuries. It was intimately connected with a new vision of the human person and the power of human reason. The effects of this development are already displayed in sixteenth-century sacramental theology.

In the post-Reformation secular sphere of philosophy, stress was placed on the power of human reason to reconstruct reality and to manipulate and change it. All was delivered up to reconstructing reason. This new rational approach is directly opposed to the old biblical and Christian understanding, which refuses to accept the notion that all reality comes under the power of reason and can be manipulated by it to serve the needs of human beings according to the principle of reason. In the old view the deepest meaning of all creation is already given by God with the creation of the world and humankind. Reality was considered to consist of hierarchically ordered beings reaching up to the mystery of God and as graduated manifestations of the mystery of God. In continuity with this Patristic viewpoint, Scholastic theologians valued sacraments as a logical consequence and high point of the symbolic dimension of all creation. Hugo of St. Victor, for example, taught that sacramental signs, on the grounds of creation, are forms of expression of grace established by God. Hence, he had a difficult time explaining the exact nature of the acts by which Christ could be said to have instituted sacraments.

The post-Reformation new understanding of the relation of human reason to reality seems to have already taken hold in an imperceptible way in the sixteenth century reflection on the institution of sacraments by Christ. On the one hand the Reformers insisted that immediate positive institution of sacraments by Christ is fundamental. Since the New Testament seems to record only an explicit word of Jesus Christ in regard to the rites of baptism and Eucharist, they generally settled for two sacraments. Catholic theologians of the Counter-Reformation placed the strong accent on the institution of all seven sacraments by Christ, while disputing over what Christ himself determined concerning the essential external rites of some sacraments.

The attempt to establish the institution of sacraments by a positive divine decree, without reference to the sacramental nature of all reality, does not correspond to the teaching of the early and high Scholastics, although they also held for the institution of sacraments by Christ. It is indicative of a lack of ability to maintain an integrated view of the real world. In a word, with the loss of a sacramental understanding of all reality, the doctrine of analogy is deprived of its grounds. This inability probably accounts, in part, for the insensitivity of the fathers of the Council of Trent towards the objection of a minority group of theologians, who petitioned that the first canon of the Decree on the Sacraments not simply condemn the opinion that the sacraments of the new law are "more or less than seven."[6]

Obviously these theologians agreed that the sacraments are at least seven in number, but they wanted to include the notion that the concept of sacrament extends beyond the seven chief rites of the Church. The narrow perception of the sacramental economy of salvation also accounts for Catholic theology's failure to recognize that the sacraments are acts of the Church itself, which, therefore, can be called a sacrament.

We have already seen that the Second Vatican Council provides a vision of the sacramental nature of the Church. It describes the sacraments as acts of the Church, which realizes itself as the sacrament of Christ in its essential activities. Still this council did not attempt to show how the Church and its sacraments might help to correct the modern experience of reality outlined above. This gap needs to be filled. For in a more radical way than in the eighteenth and nineteenth centuries, reason has been elevated to the highest principle. Human sciences, through their practice, have established the human dimensions of reality and their basic structures. Reconstructed and organized nature has become the house in which we live.

This modern context makes it difficult to experience the cosmos as open to transcendence, in manifold ways reflecting the mystery of God's grandeur. The planning, organizing reason in modern times provides a hindrance to the integrative powers of human beings. To be sure, modern humanity has not lost a sacramental understanding of the world. It still lives under the facade of enlightenment. But the perception of deeper meaning, symbolic perception, needs to be fostered. In this age of advanced industrial society, where does the liturgy fit in? How can sacraments be understood in a context in which the whole of reality is not itself generally experienced as exhibiting in some way a sacramental structure?

In the modern industrial world, which pins its hopes on human ingenuity, past is not very important, and the future is defined as the product of present planning and activity. The only hope that can be named is the capacity of human reason. Sacramental celebrations provide a different point of view. They announce that the present achievement of human development is not merely a result of human work. It is grounded on what God has done for us in the past in Jesus Christ and is bestowed on us as a gift in the present. The experience of God's saving activity in the sacraments, therefore, generates a hope which is based on the ever new possibilities of the working of the Spirit through human activity.

The sacraments offer a new orientation for human existence, which breaks through the seemingly fixed ordering of daily life and reveals it as multidimensional. The sacramental structure of all reality is thereby manifested through the sacramental celebrations themselves. As an integral part of the divine movement in history, the sacraments have the potential to broaden the Christian experience of the sacramental universe. But this effect is conditioned by the existence of stable, mature Christian communities, that really witness by daily life and liturgy that their stability is grounded on Jesus Christ.

Seven Sacraments of the Church

Within a sacramental perception of all reality, the seven sacraments appear as seven ways in which the Church, as sacrament itself, actualizes its nature as minister of Christ in the unfolding of the mission of salvation. These chief rites of the Church are related, as we have said, to seven specific and common situations of Christian life. They announce, especially through the central symbolic actions and accompanying word of faith, that God's saving presence is to be found in these situations and tell how the subjects of the sacraments are to respond.

They are called sacraments to distinguish them from other instances of ritual use that merely signify a human and social situation. A human community, as such, can only signify some human reality. On the other hand, sacraments involve God's saving activity. Incorporation into the Church is incorporation into Christ in the Spirit. It has a "we" character, which goes to the very heart of the mystery of human life, the unity of the whole human race. It is a sharing in the Spirit whom Christ possesses in fullness. That is why the mystery of the Church can be described as the common sharing of all members together in the one Spirit of Christ.

The number seven is not intended to exclude the possibility that the word of faith can be directed to a variety of situations and thereby effectively announce God's saving presence and provide the clue to a fitting response. There are limitless possibilities for "sacramental events" in daily life. Wherever the authentic Word of God is preached to others, God's personal and saving presence is realized, and if the hearer responds to it in faith, the life of union with God is deepened.

SACRAMENTS: SIGNS AND CAUSES OF GRACE

Christian faith connects celebrations of the sacraments with communication of God's grace. In baptism one is born again "of water and the Spirit" (John 3:5). Through sharing of the Eucharistic bread and cup, the community is united to the crucified and Risen Lord (1 Cor 10:16) and to one another in Christ (1 Cor 10:17). But what is the relation between what the community does in the liturgy and the grace effect which occurs simultaneously? How are we to approach the understanding of the sacraments' role in mediating the communication of divine life in Christ through the Spirit?

Traditional Scholastic theology begins from above, with the divine act, and attempts to integrate the ecclesiastical act into the sacramental grace event. This is done by situating the minister of the sacrament on the side of God or Christ and on the side of the Church. The minister is described as acting in the place of Christ. More frequently now the term "in the person of Christ" (*in persona Christi*) is used in official Church documents to stress that the minister represents Christ as a real symbol, that is, Christ acts through the ministerial act. Correspondingly, the liturgy of the sacraments is understood to contain a rite: a symbolic gesture and sacramental word instituted by Christ, at least as far as its significa-tion. When the minister performs this rite, he represents Christ vis-à-vis the recipient of the sacrament.

The minister also represents the Church in the sacramental cele-bration. He does this by reciting the liturgical prayers and carry-ing out the ritual actions which surround the essential sacramental rite. In addition the Church enters into the realization of the essen-tial sacramental rite by providing the correct form which corre-sponds to the will of Christ and by specifying its meaning. Hence, the minister must follow the lead of Church tradition in order to administer a true sacrament. For the sacraments have been entrusted to the Church and not to the minister independently of the Church. This condition is formulated in the traditional expression that the minister must have the intention "to do what the Church does" (*fa-ciendi quod facit ecclesia*).

To do what the Church does can mean simply that the minister must perform the ritual act deemed essential by the Church. Whether this minimum intention, this correct performance of the rite, is suf-ficient for the realization of a valid sacramental rite is open to debate. Especially since the post-Reformation period Catholic theologians have more commonly argued that the sacrament is invalid if the minister secretly intends not to administer a sacrament.

The need for the minister to perform the essential rite prescribed by the Church ultimately is based on the need to follow the will of Christ known to the Church in faith. So the formula, "to do what the Church does," can be reduced to "to do what Christ wills to be done" in the celebration of his sacraments. This would not be done, of course, if the minister publicly disavowed the intention to celebrate a sacrament. The further condition, that the minister does not exclude the goal of the celebration by a secret intention, can be formulated positively as "to intend to do what the Church intends to do through the celebration." Ultimately, it means "to intend what Christ intends."

This doctrine of intention establishes a weak link between the minister of the sacrament and the Church. The Church, or rather the traditional teaching and practice of the Church, supplies the knowledge of what must be done in the celebration if it is to be conformed to the will of Christ. To the extent that the minister can invalidate the sacrament by a secret intention, the rest of the community can claim the sacrament as its own only in virtue of the fact that its official ministry has the power to represent Christ.

The new ecclesiological turn of sacramental theology has resulted in a more nuanced approach to the relation between the minister of the sacrament and both Christ and the Church. Sacraments are now viewed as acts of the Church as such, not merely acts of the minister of Christ in the Church, to whose hierarchy the sacraments have been entrusted. This means that the local gathered community, which represents and realizes the Church of Christ in space and time, is the direct subject of the liturgical act under the leadership of its ordained minister. This minister, therefore, is more clearly seen as both the representative of the Church and Christ in all aspects of the liturgical celebration. Consequently, it becomes less evident that the presiding minister alone can invalidate the rite by a secret intention. Furthermore, the sharp distinction between what the minister does in the liturgy exclusively in the person of Christ (that is, the essential sacramental rite) and what the minister does in the person of the Church (that is, the rest of the liturgical prayer and symbolic actions) becomes questionable. Rather, the minister, by virtue of his ordination, appears to be, in all liturgical activity, the representative of Christ, because he represents the community of which Christ is the head. The correctness of this viewpoint becomes evident when one realizes that even the so-called essential matter and form of the sacraments are the expression of the faith of the Church which always corresponds to the will of Christ, who, in the Spirit, is the living source of that faith.

The local community, as such, is the real symbol of Christ in its sacramental activity realized under the leadership of a qualified minister who, according to traditional teaching, must be ordained—except in certain cases such as emergency baptism and matrimony. When the local Church expresses itself, it necessarily expresses and mediates the grounds of its being, Christ in the Spirit, not withstanding any inward disavowal of its liturgical leader. Therefore, it realizes through its activity a grace event in favor of the subjects of the sacraments. However, the question is still left open: what concept of causality can be used to shed light on the mode of communication of the new sacramental grace which occurs in the celebration?

The more recent approach of a theology from above employs the model of transient efficient causality in a new way. It accepts the old principle that sacraments both signify and cause grace. But it brings together the two functions in such a way that the signifying and causal functions are not opposed to one another. In short, it employs the model of causality of sign: sacraments cause by signifying.

In this systematic approach, which corresponds in part to that of St. Thomas Aquinas, sacraments have an effect analogous to that of human signs. Both produce an effect of the intentional order. Sacraments cause knowledge by manifesting the divine will to sanctify the subject of the sacrament. But this effect goes beyond that of the intentional order. Because God is the author of all being and the relations of being, a real relation is established by the divine will between the external rite and the sacramental grace bestowed on the recipient. The grace of the sacrament is not in the sign, except by extrinsic denomination; grace is in the person, justified or more deeply sanctified. But there is always a real offer of grace through the sacramental signs, because God has established them as signs of grace. Since grace is linked to the sign through the real relation established by God, and the grace received depends on the response in faith to the sign for its actualization, the sign can be called an instrumental cause of grace.

This theological analysis recalls certain basic principles. First, sanctification of human beings takes place in and through historical forms of communication, of which sacraments are paradigms. Second, sacramental celebrations are new grace events. Moreover, it presupposes that sacramental celebrations have a transcendental dimension. This means that grace, understood as the Holy Spirit sent to a person in the economy of salvation from the Father, is a transcendental act, that is, it emanates from God in God's pure divinity. As such, the communication of grace is immediate; it is not filtered through a human symbolic action. On the other hand, this theological approach recognizes that the human being, constitutively ordained to the Trinity and aspiring to union with the

Trinity, must perceive the offer of divine self-communication in order to accept it personally and, being affirmed by God as other, grow in the unity of love.

All grace events are unique and historical. Historical forms of this encounter are not a medium of God's self-communication as such. Rather, they play a mediating role, in that they enable the person to accept God's offer of loving communion in a personal way. However, the modes of sacramental communication between God and creatures are not always the same. Above all, they cannot be simply reduced to an abstract theory of causality of sign and divine power, as is done in the systematic approach described above. In the case of sacraments of the Church, one must take account of the ecclesial dimension. From the viewpoint of the liturgist, the symbolized reality—God's self-communication, proportionate to the purpose of each sacrament—is so intimately connected with the sacramental rite that it can be approached as reality only through the rite as act of the believing community.[7]

The Liturgical Community

The introduction of the community of believers into the explanation of the efficacy of the sacraments is required because the ritual celebration is an act in which the whole community is a potentially active subject. This element was not sufficiently integrated into the traditional approach since the high Middle Ages, which concentrated on the activity of the Trinity, the incarnate and Risen Lord, the minister of Christ as official representative of the whole Church, and the rite itself as instituted by Christ to confer the grace it signifies. Here the community of believers as such is viewed as participating in the liturgical act indirectly through the official representatives.

As act of the Church, the liturgy pertains to the category of religious cult, that is, the distinctive form of expression of the governing interests and value relations of a religious culture. Within the coherence of images, rules of conduct, and language based on the vision of faith, the participants of the liturgy are enabled to identify themselves, to take their stand within the community, and to participate in the experience of faith of the community.

Liturgy provides a particular instance of intercommunication between Christians in the form of stylized expression of the life of faith of the Church. It is not an example of a dramatic play on a stage, a dramatic presentation exhibiting a message to an audience with which the audience identifies vicariously. Rather, it is an action in which all those present are potentially active subjects. On the other hand, liturgy is not an instance of a human and social event limited to the human dimension. It involves a deeper spiritual meaning.

The deeper spiritual reality that is lived is that of mutual love: love of God and love of the participants. It is the reality of reciprocal love made possible because of God's radical self-communication to all human existence. It has two aspects, a divine offer of personal communion and a human response of self-offering made possible by the indwelling presence of the Spirit of Christ. The effect of this indwelling of the Holy Spirit is knowledge of what is really being offered and the capacity to accept it as the grounds of the fulfillment of human existence.

The offer of personal communion in the grace events of the liturgy of the sacraments is total on the side of God; it is not total on the side of believers. First, they are not able to make a decision which holds once and for all in their condition of historical existence. Second, the capacity for openness to God's personal offer of loving communion is determined by detachment from self-seeking and self-justification.

Under the conditions of historical existence, human beings are ordered to a limitless openness to receive the meaning of their lives from God. The term of this openness is attained only by Jesus Christ. No other human being so enjoys the ultimate depth of intimacy of the loving union with the Father except the historical Jesus. No other human being attains the freedom to respond to the fullest depth of human capacity to the offer of God's self-communication, except the Incarnate Word.

All human beings, moreover, must express their openness to God's love by incarnating it in their human activity. There is no other way that believers, under the condition of historical existence, can express their love of God, for they are spirit in body. The full expression of their love of God must include the expression of love for all of God's creatures. This was also the way in which Jesus Christ expressed his love of the Father up to his self-offering on the Cross for the many.

On the other hand, there is no other means of God's personal self-communication to believers which corresponds to their actual nature, except human communication. Human communication through culture is the condition for human development at all levels.

Correspondingly, God's personal self-communication takes place in visible, tangible form in all cultures and periods of history through human interpersonal communication. In its highest form it occurs in the Incarnate Word (John 1:14-18). Through the Church, in turn, "God's manifold wisdom is made known . . . in accord with his age-old purpose, carried out in Christ Jesus our Lord" (Eph 3:10-11). This means through the ministry of believers to one another. What Paul says of his own ministry is applicable to all believers in accord with their various gifts (Eph 3:8-9). While God's personal self-giving through history is as broad as the variety of forms of human communication, it is realized in its highest personal forms in the historical Jesus and in the exercise of the faith of Christians.

Within the Church liturgy provides a particular instance of this intercommunication in the form of a condensed, stylized representation of the daily life of the faith. For example, the rite of baptism signifies a human and social reality, the offer of membership by the community and the acceptance by the neophyte. This, in turn, signifies for the eyes of faith incorporation into the Body of Christ by the gift of the Spirit and bestowal of the new life which enables the living out of the way of Christ. The rite of penance signifies a new engagement of the sinner in the life of the Church and the renewal of the community's commitment to support the sinner. The human and social reality is mutual reconciliation. This signifies reconciliation with God in Christ, the head of the Church. There are not two completely distinct forms of reconciliation. Rather, reconciliation with God comes through the form of reconciliation with the Church. The act of the community, through its representative, and that of the penitent form one true act which becomes a new beginning to be unfolded in daily life, supported by the deeper reconciliation with God which is simultaneously realized because Christ in the Spirit is the source of the human reconciliation.

Sacraments and Faith of the Church

The objective faith of the Church is expressed in the fixed forms of the sacramental celebrations of particular groups of Christians. Since this faith is personally incarnated only in the faith of individual believers, it is not personally present if the group as a whole is without faith. In such a situation, difficult to imagine, the liturgy of the sacraments remains the expression of the faith of the Church, objectivized in the language and symbolic action. It has the capacity to draw out the subjective response of a believer. But if no one has real, active faith, the purpose of the sacrament is frustrated. The historical expression of the Church's faith remains without a concrete subject in the act of worship.

As the expression of the faith of the Church, the sacraments signify the belief that the grace of Christ is being offered, for example: "I baptize you in the name of the Father, Son, and Holy Spirit." At the same time the whole liturgy indicates the response which is expected of the participants. One thinks of the Eucharistic Prayer, which offers praise and thanksgiving for what the Father has done and is doing for us through his Son. Insofar as the sacramental rites point to God's activity, they realize what they signify precisely because they are the expression of the faith of the whole Church. In other words, what the sacraments affirm as conviction of faith, that God is offering grace, is ultimately based on the indwelling presence of the Spirit in the Church who inspires the Church to make this claim. Insofar as the liturgy of the sacraments signifies the grateful response of the participants, it does not automatically realize what it signifies. Why? Because it presupposes that the participants agree with this offer of grace. But this is something which cannot be simply guaranteed. One can pay lip service, while not worshipping in the heart.

This structure of the sacramental celebrations indicates that the communication of grace cannot be described on the model of physical instrumental causality, the model of instrument of art. In the case of instruments of art, the instrument is placed over against the object being acted on by the principal cause, for example, the brush used to paint a picture. However, the sacraments are precisely a human activity in which the faith of the Church is expressed. They cannot be placed vis-á-vis the celebrating community. Rather, they objectively express the faith of the Church and that of the community gathered, to the extent that it agrees with the fixed forms of the liturgy. Consequently, it is through the human language and symbolic actions by which the community expresses itself that God's self-communication takes place and is received in a fruitful way.

All this points to the fact that the sacraments are paradigms of the way in which God communicates self to humanity in history. God always gives self through human language and symbolic actions. In the measure that God offers self in and through human communication, in human events and human fellowship, one speaks of a concentration of sacramentality. In the measure that the Creator engages self concretely and personally, so as to identify with the fate of a people or individual person, the action of God makes the human life process sacramental. According to the degree of the personal coming of God, God's coming-into-play, the historical activity of human beings becomes more intensely sacramental. At the high point of this sacramental communication, must be placed the seven sacraments. For here, in a most concentrated way, the faith of the whole Church is expressed, which always manifests and realizes God's saving activity in its essential acts.

Celebration of the Whole Community

All the sacraments have the form of a dialogue between God in Christ and the Church. They announce the offer of grace to the individual, and relate this person to the community in a special way. The faith of the whole Church is expressed through the rites, and the gathered community expresses this faith as its own through the communication between the participants. Because of the various roles of the participants, there is a giving and receiving. This human dialogue signifies, for the eyes of faith, a dialogue between Christ and the Church. For Christ in the Spirit is the source of this human dialogue. So the human giving and receiving ultimately represent God as the giver and the community as only the receiver of saving grace. Therefore, the community can only be identified as giver insofar as it ministerially offers the grace of God to one another through the proclamation of the Gospel by verbal and ritual preaching. That is why the liturgy of the sacraments is ultimately directed to God: a response of praise and thanksgiving for what God has done and is now doing in the act of worship. In the end it is God alone who gives the grace.

Since sacraments are, first of all, a celebration of the faith of the Church by an ecclesial community, they are a proclamation of the offer of God's self-communication made to the whole community. They express the faith of the Church that the community as such, in its members, is the subject of God's love. By agreeing with this faith of the Church, the members of the community become more fully open to receive the one Spirit whom Christ possesses in fullness. They grow into the maturity of the Body of Christ through the sharing of the gifts they have received.

Apart from the Eucharist, in which the sacrament of the Body and Blood of Christ is intended to be shared with all the participants, other sacramental celebrations take place in favor of an individual. Here a special proclamation of the personal offer of God's love is directed to the particular subjects. The whole community does not share in this offer of God's grace directly, for it is made to the individual. But the community shares indirectly by its grateful agreement with the grace being offered to one of its members. In this way the community is drawn to recognize its responsibility towards the individual subject of the sacrament and, through its thankful response, obtains the spiritual help to be a support for that person's growth in the life of faith. Moreover, the community is made aware that all saving grace is the gift of God—as manifested in the sacramental offer of God's personal communication. So, giving thanks for the life of faith granted to it, the community opens itself to receive a deepening of the personal grasp of life in Christ.

Offer of Grace to the Individual Subject

The individual comes to the sacramental celebration with a personal faith commitment. But in the liturgy one does not merely express thanksgiving for what has been experienced as the gift of grace elsewhere. The sacramental celebration does not merely serve as a kind of instrument for the participant to give external expression to the grateful dispositions which one brings to the liturgy. Rather, through the celebration the subject of the sacrament is both offered grace and, through liturgical language and symbolic actions, is given the gift to agree with this offer by gratefully acknowledging that it is a gift given apart from personal merit.

The sacraments announce that grace transcends the personal commitment of the one who expresses one's faith. This faith itself is a gift. Hence, the individual subject is helped by the sacrament. Participating in the expression of the objective faith of the community, the individual is enabled to transcend one's personal faith commitment and to experience the offer of grace and accept it with thanksgiving. This is something which the individual is incapable of doing for oneself. No one can make a sacrament for oneself.

Specific Efficacy of Sacraments

In daily life truly human activity takes place through the engagement of the whole self with the surrounding environment and other human beings. Through the encounter one is often led to an uplifting experience. For example, when one sits on a hillside in autumn and looks at the marvelous variety of colors of the leaves of trees touched by the frost, the result is an experience of beauty. The attentive reading of the Bible often ends in an experience of truth and confidence in God. This experience does not have its profound cause in the human engagement itself. It comes as a gift. The human work simply leads to the experience.

The indissoluble link between the human act and the humanizing experience which happens to us is also found in the life of faith. The engagement of faith in the daily life of service of the neighbor results in the experience of the loving God working through us to support the other in need and, in the measure of the response of the other to our service, we experience God's love for us. Whether it be routine living or liturgical celebrations, the experience of salvation comes as a gift which is measured by the depth of the personal engagement.

According to the traditional teaching of the Church, there is an intimate relationship between the active participation in the sacraments and the personal sharing in God's self-communication. Since it is a question of a personal giving on the part of God and a personal receiving on the part of the believer, the openness to God's grace measures the depth of the event of sanctification. The personal engagement of one's faith is the condition for the personal reception of God's grace.

Scholastic theology rightly stresses that the experience of being really graced by God is not a matter of human activity. God's self-communication is God's work! However, the concern to stress the preeminence of God's activity in the sacraments led to a theory of sacramental signs which placed them completely on God's side vis-à-vis the community. God is described as having instituted sacraments through Christ and placed them at the disposal of the Church to use for the benefit of the faithful. They are depicted as objective means of grace, standing on their own in the liturgical rite, which otherwise expresses the faith of the Church.

The fatal flaw in this presentation lies in the sharp distinction made between the liturgical spheres of the expression of God's love and the response of the Church. However, it can be shown that the essential signs of the sacraments—the so-called matter and form of the sacraments—are an expression of the faith of the Church. The whole New Testament is the record of the faith of original Christian communities, grounded on the preaching of the original witnesses of the resurrection of Jesus Christ. Therefore, the essential rites of the sacraments are the liturgical expression of the faith of the Church. For they are based on the witness of faith, which is recorded in the New Testament. The various accounts of the institution of the Eucharist, for example, go back to the Last Supper. But in the forms we find them in the New Testament, they are expressions of the faith of the Church formulated according to the Church's understanding of the meaning of its celebration of the Lord's Supper.

A closer look at the elements of the sacramental celebrations shows that they consist in human language and corporeal expression, constructed by the human activity of the Church under the inspiration of the Spirit. They correspond to and express the faith of the Church. The language of the sacraments transmits knowledge of a relationship between God and the believers. It announces that God's grace is being communicated for the benefit of the participants. Hence, the intention of this language is to transform the worship situation and to carry the community to a new level of religious experience. In short it is intended to disclose the mystery of God's presence and so enable a proper response. This liturgical language represents an instance of the transformative function of the timely word, such as that described in the account of the experience of the disciples occasioned by the conversation with the Risen Lord on the road to Emmaus: "Were not our hearts burning inside us as he talked" (Luke 24:32).

This language of the sacraments is performative speech. It is not aimed only at providing information about what God has done in the past. Hence, it cannot be explained as merely a means by which the participants of the liturgy recount what they have already experienced in the life of faith. Rather, it announces what God is doing now in the form of a summons to accept it with thanksgiving. The speech of the sacraments expresses the confidence of faith that Christ is present and acting in the Spirit, even to giving himself personally as crucified and Risen Lord in the bread and wine of the Eucharist.

Since the sacraments are the expression of the faith of the Church, it follows that the efficacy of the celebrations for the individual adult depends on the integration of one's subjective commitment of faith into the liturgical expression of the Church's faith. If the participants do not agree with the faith of the Church expressed in the liturgy, there is no possibility of a personal engagement with God in the liturgy according to the conditions expressed in the liturgy itself. If the participants agree, then they are carried along and supported by the sacrament to respond appropriately to God in Christ.

The whole purpose of the sacraments is to enable the gathered community to become in act what it is by its very nature, the Body of Christ. The goal of the communication of grace, according to the whole tradition, is no more nor less than to make people human subjects who are freed from the narrow confines of their own understanding of themselves, to realize that they are called to be answering subjects of God's offer of loving communion. This grace of God attains its finality when the Spirit so penetrates the bones and marrow of the Christian that he or she can take their stand over against the God of love and respond in love with the whole Church. The ideal liturgy is one in which all the participants of the liturgical act identify with the authentic faith. Here the word of the last chapter of the Book of Revelation can serve as a description of the liturgy of the saints: "The Spirit and the Bride say, 'Come!' Let him who hears answer, 'Come!' Let him who is thirsty come forward; let all who desire it accept the gift of life-giving water" (Rev 22:17).

The sacraments enable the community as a whole to become an active subject responding to God and the individual subjects to identify themselves and take their proper place in the community of faith. For this human expression of faith of the sacraments has Christ in the Spirit as its living source. The kernel of the sacramental rites is not a means of grace over against the participants. It does not take the form of a miraculous appearance of God's saving presence or an objective institutional means to be used by the Church in favor of the individuals. Rather, it is the incarnation of grace in the form of the liturgical expression of the faith of the Church itself.

As expression of the objective faith of the Church, of which Christ in the Spirit is the source, the sacraments mediate the disposition of the subject to respond to God's grace. By agreeing with this faith, the individual is made fully a subject of the sacramental celebration, not a passive object of the sacramental bestowal of grace. Hence, God's grace appears as granting the disposition to the subject of the sacrament to respond to God's offer of grace. As forms of communication of the faith of the Church, sacraments bestow grace and bring the faith of the individual to a new and higher level, enabling a deeper integration into the life of the Body of Christ. But all of this, of course, is conditioned by the effort of the individual, under the inspiration of the Spirit, to be involved seriously in the celebration of the sacraments.

Conclusion

Through the sacramental celebrations the Church experiences the saving presence of God. Consequently, it recalls its foundation in the liturgical prayer: the redemptive work of Christ and the sending of the Spirit to draw the believers into communion with the Father through Christ. At the same time the Church is aware that, since the final age has come, Christ is actively present in the Spirit in a new way in all situations of the lives of Christians and all others. Hence, the Church makes no sharp distinction between the spheres of the holy and profane. To the extent it is recognized that Christ is present in all situations of life calling for the decision of faith in the loving God, the liturgy of the Church appears in a new light.

The Church's liturgy of the sacraments is not the only place where Christ is to be found with his saving grace. Moreover, Christ's presence in the whole range of human life points to the time when humanity will no longer require the special moments of communal worship. In the transformed world of the kingdom of God, the people of God will continually commune with the Trinity in "Spirit and truth" (John 4:23). However, in the age of the Church, the variety of holy encounters with the Lord in daily life do not suffice to meet the needs of a full life of faith. Christians need to be continually supported by the community of faith. They cannot do without the liturgy in which they renew and deepen their personal faith by expressing and enlarging on it within the scope of the expression of the faith of the whole Church.

Footnotes

1. Edward Schillebeeckx, *Christ, The Sacrament of the Encounter with God* (New York: Sheed & Ward, 1963).

2. Karl Rahner, *The Church and the Sacraments* (New York: Herder & Herder, 1963).

3. *Vatican Council II: The Conciliar and Post Conciliar Documents*, ed. A. Flannery, (Collegeville, Minn.: The Liturgical Press, 1975) 1-36.

4. *Ibid.*

5. E.J. Kilmartin, "A Modern Approach to the Word of God and the Sacraments of Christ: Perspectives and Principles," *The Sacraments: God's Love and Mercy Actualized*, ed. F. A. Eigo (Philadelphia: Villanova University, 1979) 73-77.

6. *Ibid.*

7. F. Tillmans, "The Sacraments as Symbolical Reality of Faith," *Fides Sacramenti Sacramentum Fidei*, eds. H. J. Auf der Maur, et al. (Assen, the Netherlands: Van Gorcum, 1981) 253-276.

Selected References

Casel, Odo. *The Mystery of Christian Worship.* Westminster, Md.: Newman Press, 1962. The most concise presentation of the author's understanding of Christian liturgy as the actualization of the mystery presence of Christ and his redemptive work.

Duffy, Regis. A. *Real Presence.* New York: Harper & Row, 1982. Analysis of the subjective side of sacramental celebrations, the engagement of the faith of the participants.

Flannery, Austin, ed. *Vatican Council II: The Conciliar and Post Conciliar Documents.* Collegeville, Minn.: The Liturgical Press, 1975. Besides the conciliar documents this volume contains the more important Vatican publications relating to the conciliar decrees. Twenty-four documents concerning the implementation of the Constitution on the Sacred Liturgy are included.

Foley, Leonard. *Signs of Love.* St. Anthony Messenger Press, 1976. An explanation of the sacraments which takes as the point of departure the revised rites of the Roman Catholic Church.

Keating, Charles. *Christian Sacraments and Christian Growth.* Twenty-Third Publications, 1976. Sacraments are considered as revelatory of deeper dimensions of human development.

Kilmartin, Edward J. "A Modern Approach to the Word of God and the Sacraments of Christ: Perspectives and Principles," in Francis A. Eigo, ed. *The Sacraments: God's Love and Mercy Actualized.* Philadelphia: Villanova University, 1979, 59–109.

Lee, Bernard. *The Beginning of the Church.* New York: Paulist Press, 1974. Analysis of the religious experience of sacramental events using the concepts and categories of process philosophy.

McCauley, George. *Sacraments for the Secular Man.* New York: Herder & Herder, 1969. Analysis of the sacramental symbolism as it relates to basic human values of the life of faith.

Powers, Joseph. *Spirit and Sacrament.* Minneapolis: Seabury, 1983. Addresses the question of the meaning of sacrament by showing how the symbolism connects with various dimensions of the human experience of transcendence.

Rahner, Karl. *The Church and the Sacraments.* New York: Herder & Herder, 1963. A short but very important contribution to the understanding of the Church as sacrament which opens the way to a new approach to traditional themes of sacramental theology.

Rahner, Karl. *Meditations on the Sacraments.* Minneapolis: Seabury, 1977. Prayerful reflections on the seven sacraments based on this theologian's vision of the whole economy of salvation.

Schillebeeckx, Edward H. *Christ, the Sacrament of the Encounter with God.* Sheed & Ward, 1963. A personalistic approach to the sacraments set in the context of traditional Thomistic sacramental theology.

Semmelroth, Otto. *Church and Sacraments.* Notre Dame, Ind.: Fides, 1965. A succinct theological explanation of the relationship between Christ, Church, and the sacraments of the Church.

Worgul, George. *From Magic to Metaphor.* New York: Paulist Press, 1980. An outline of a theology of the sacraments against the background of the contribution which human sciences have made to the role of ritual in human life.

Index